BET ON YOU

Secretly, in almost everyone's heart of hearts they want to become a superhero. This book will tell you how to be all you can be, do all you can do, and have all you can have. Happy reading.
—Mark Victor Hansen, co-creator of *Chicken Soup for the Soul, One Minute Millionaire*, and *Ask!*

This book will leave you smiling, surprised and empowered with new skills that can help you live the life of your dreams.
—John Gray, best-selling relationship author of *Men Are from Mars, Women Are from Venus*

Laban, bravo for your unabashed bravery to dive deeply into your distorted reality and reveal your soul and exorcism to us! Your vulnerability and willingness to give us every detail of your recovery is cathartic for everyone who reads your poetic and painful prose. What a story and life of transformation that you've shared with us thrill seekers craving an exciting and scary literary journey. Thank you for your audacity and authenticity in this masterful expression of a life reinvented. Bravo, Laban. Bravo!
—Mark Schulman, CSP, Drummer for P!NK, Speaker, Author

Laban is connected to the energy that creates worlds. In his masterpiece, Bet on You, *Laban brings an artful eloquence in translating his experiences into writing. Vivid, colorful, and multifarious, his stories are instantly accessible and deeply uplifting.*

— Dr. Alan D. Thompson, Former Chairman, Mensa International's gifted families committee and AI Consultant at Life Architect

An absolutely riveting tale of persevering when all the odds are against you. Ditchburn is a gifted storyteller and he doesn't hold back at all in Bet on You - unveiling some of his deepest and darkest moments. This is one of the most inspiring books that I've ever read and it gives some practical life lessons on how to invest in yourself.
— Shawn Kanungo, Disruption Strategist

Inside each of us lies a superhero, and sometimes it takes a whole lot of life's lessons and experiences to recognize that superhero and let it fly. Through Laban sharing his life stories with refreshing rawness and honesty, you feel inspired to connect with your own truths and, in doing so, the superhero lying within is revealed.
— Monica Rosenfeld, INcredible Communication keynote speaker and founder of the Broadcast Your Book PR System

This book is a fascinating insight to a fellow man's journey through what can only be described as hell and back. The story has been told with a rawness and honesty that makes you feel like you are part of the whole thing. Laban's insights also provide us with some powerful wisdom along the way. He should be commended and thanked for sharing his story with us all.
— Sir Steve Hansen, Former coach of the world champion

New Zealand All Blacks and 4 x World Rugby Coach of the year.

If you're looking for a book that immediately grabs you by the %&$# and takes you on a wild journey of personal reflection and big life lessons, then this is the book for you. Bet on You is a "can't put it down" read right from the start. Laban's stories and life lessons show each of us that our path of infinite possibilities becomes clear when we stop playing small and go all in on the one person that matters most - you. Do your future self a favor and buy this book today!
—Evans Putman, Creator of The Servepreneur Blueprint and leader of the Servepreneur Movement

Laban Ditchburn is a great story teller and his own story is the best one of all.
—Professor Peter Brukner OAM, MBBS, FACSP Sport and Exercise Medicine Physician

BET ON YOU

Laban Ditchburn

SUMMIT PRESS
Publishers

Printed in the United States of America

First Printing, 2021

ISBN: 978-0-9863309-9-5

Summit Press Publishers

411 Walnut Street # 12515

Green Cove Springs, FL 32043-3443

author@summit-success.com

Quantity sales. Special discounts are available on quantity purchases by corporations, associations, and others.

For details, contact author@summit-success.com

DEDICATION

This book was gifted to me by a force far greater than I'll ever be able to explain.

I dedicate this book to its rightful recipient... you.

CONTENTS

FOREWORD

You've got something special… you've got GREATNESS in you!

If you've heard me speak or have followed my career, you know that I believe each of us is born with special gifts and a unique value that we can share with the world. I call that our greatness and it's powerful and real. There's no greater feeling than tapping into that greatness and living your life from that place.

The problem is that many of us have hidden traumas, secrets, shame, and guilt that we carry inside. All of those emotions mixed with unhealed pain create blocks within us that can prevent us from ever truly connecting with our innate and God-given gift of greatness.

If you have ever been in this place, or you find yourself there now, you're not alone. Most of us have been there. There was a time in my life when I was disconnected and in *Bet on You*, Laban Michael Ditchburn reveals that holding on to his own personal pain deeply stunted his growth as well. Laban found himself lost and languishing in a life that didn't serve him. He was betting on everything else in his world to bring him "fortune" without realizing that he was making the ultimate wager… sacrificing his greatness.

In this gritty, honest, and raw read, Laban shows his amazing transformation from addiction to accepting help and how he fought hard to reach a place of enlightenment from darkness. *Bet on You* is a portal to self-awareness where you'll learn how Laban took charge of his mind, stopped living life as a liability, and transformed into a powerful asset and change agent in the world.

I am inspired by Laban's story and by his passion to encourage others to bet on themselves and release themselves from the bondage of their past.

If you find yourself in a place of confusion and indecision, I encourage you to Bet on You. Sometimes it's your only option and as Laban shows, it works.

That's my story, and I'm sticking to it!

Yours in GREATNESS,

Les Brown
Author, Speaker, Trainer

MY TWO QUEENS

"Why don't you take us home and we'll let you do *an-y-thing you want?*" she whispered.

A puff of warm breath from the "t" in *want* activated the erogenous zone in my lips.

The eastern bloc accent made me think of Bond girls.

"But of course."

They were physically perfect and smelled like strawberries.

Tall, athletic, olive skinned, and brunette, with super long eyelashes that fluttered in my direction.

Hair up, but more than long enough to travel past their perfect derrieres.

Their red, knee-high Louboutins fitted with sparkling diamantes sent rainbows of light in every direction.

I was voluntarily trapped on a huge chesterfield sofa with two of the most beautiful women I had ever seen.

Double and Trouble they called themselves, preferring mystique and anonymity.

They were entrepreneurs of the highest order and I had just been offered the ultimate *indecent proposal.*

"And what would my investment be?" I asked. My shoulders tensed into my neck with anticipation of their response.

"Two thousand-dollars... cash," Trouble said.

"Anything you want."

Remaining cool like an Alaskan winter, I responded with feigned nonchalance.

"Ladies, ladies, ladies... you've seen what I've spent tonight; I couldn't pay that much if I wanted to!"

Two pals visiting from overseas, another local friend and I had decided a gentleman's club would be our home for the evening.

Like soldiers released on shore leave, we steam-trained into that place with blood alcohol levels high enough to blind most amateurs.

We needed a quick chemical intervention to level out the intoxication.

A chance encounter with a fellow patron provided us exactly what we needed.

Sporting a traditional ponytail, buffalo-leather vest, and more tassels than Dolly Parton's wardrobe, he looked to be a legitimate Native American.

I stood alongside him at the men's urinal and channelled my inner *Geronimo*.

"How," I said, using my lowest octave and raising my right hand to show I held no weapon and meant no harm.

My left hand remained attached to my own "weapon," as urinating on another man's shoes is never cool at the best of times.

He was as high as a kite, and he knew that I knew.

"What do you need?" he bellowed in an even deeper voice, his accent confirming my guess.

"Drugs, please?" I enquired.

He grinned, zipped up his fly, and within sixty seconds, I had exchanged cash for a fun-sized Ziploc bag of dusty green pills.

They had the Mitsubishi logo pressed into them (a.k.a. "Green Mitzis," for all you retired ravers) and looked real enough.

It's astonishing the reckless levels of confidence I placed in drug dealers when it came to consuming illicit substances (mind you, I did the same with the legal stuff and you'll soon find how well that turned out)!

Without further thought, I gulped down two pills, room temperature whiskey my only lubricant.

I shuddered uncomfortably as the alcohol attacked my central nervous system and carried the mystery chemical cocktail down my gullet and into my stomach.

Thirty minutes later, I was fuelled by top-shelf spirits, huge amounts of dopamine, and Christ only knows what else.

Sweat poured from my forehead and my face distorted into a lip-chewing, human-hybrid, lizard-person—something between a troll and a goblin.

A Troblin?

My pleasure receptors lit up like the Fourth of July and a river of sexual energy cascaded into my loins.

If you've ever taken MDMA, you'll empathise.

If not, imagine the best orgasm you've ever had.

Now, fall in love with everybody you meet.

Now, win the lottery. And you're still not even close.

The pleasure extends the entire length of your body and doesn't finish for hours.

Sounds awesome, hey?

The aftereffects, however, make suicide seem like a real and viable option.

When sober, I craved the feminine touch; but pump me full of a man-made love drug and I became hornier than a short-nosed fruit bat.[1]

Speaking of fruit, from the blur of my intoxication, the strawberry scented Double and Trouble both appeared.

"Hello, handsome."

Intoxicated by their scent, charm, and seduction, it was less than sixty seconds before I was led down to the "dungeon."

The special section of the club was designed for you to lose yourself. One lap dance became two, three became four, and four made it the most expensive night I'd ever had.

Draining the nearby cash machine, I quickly maxed out

---

[1] During copulation, the female short-nosed fruit bat will bend over and perform fellatio on the male while still engaged in coitus—bravo!

my daily limit of $1,000.

So, that $2,000 cash they mentioned? Impossible.

My mates didn't have it; nor did I—and even if I did, I couldn't access that much cash.

"Make it $1,600. That's our final offer," Double countered.

"Done! Give me thirty minutes, ladies."

"Sure thing, lover boy." They both grinned.

I didn't have the $1,600 needed, but I had $800 and I knew how to get the rest.

The strip-club was located half a mile from Crown Casino, Australia's flagship gambling venue.

That was my new destination and I made it in record time.

As the clock struck midnight a new day reset, and so did my withdrawal limit.

I checked my bank balance: $800.

"WITHDRAW?"

"YES."

Like Dustin Hoffman in "Rain Man," I calmly entered the gaming floor via the escalator, spied the high rollers room, and beelined straight to the blackjack table. I definitely, definitely knew what I was doing.

Here's a crash course if you've never played blackjack:

Each player is dealt two cards, individually, face up.

The dealer is also dealt two cards, one exposed and one hidden.

The value of cards two through ten is their face value.

Jack, Queen, and King are all worth ten.

Aces can be worth one or eleven.

A hand's value is the sum of the card values.

The dealer then reveals the hidden card and must draw cards, one by one, until the cards total up to seventeen points.

At seventeen points or higher, the dealer must stop.

Players bet on the basis that they will individually have better hands than the dealer.

As I traded my cash for eight $100 chips, nerves forced me to stand, rather than sit.

The dealer pushed the pile towards me, and I carefully pushed the pile back, resting them perfectly into the felt box.

I had just laid the single biggest bet of my life in order to get laid.

That would have been funny if the situation wasn't so tense.

All I needed was one result in my favor and I'd have the resources to fund a hedonistic rampage that would make Hugh Hefner blush.

Shit, I was about to engage in every man's fantasy.

Were these two willing and beautiful women a gift from a God I didn't yet believe in, but who obviously believed in me?

The power I felt placing such a large bet was simply magnificent.

Even on such a high-limit table, the whites of everyone's eyes added even more light to an already well-illuminated room.

With the final wagers placed, the dealer waved her hand across the table and affirmed, "No more bets."

As she finished her sentence, the irony of the situation hit.

I had already blown a thousand dollars on the night; now I was risking $800 to try and win $1,600, to pay for something that, had I just cut to the chase at the very start of the evening, would have saved me all that mucking about.

"Fuck," I bemused. *Why do I make my life so complicated?*

The game commenced and the blackjack began.

"Queen!" I yelled violently, slapping my hand on the table.

That's ten, I counted in my head.

The croupier dealt her own cards and delivered a King of Spades.

Her second card was placed face-down, hidden from everyone's view.

My heartbeat was already racing from my sprint to the casino complex; now it had more beats per minute than nineties techno.

The second round of cards arrived and to my utter delight another Queen arrived.

"Yes!" I exclaimed aloud.

My yell scared the crap out of the craps table and the mahjong from the mahjongers.

The dealer delivered the rest of the cards in silence and the remaining gamblers surrounding me all went bust.

I could feel them silently wishing unimaginable harm to

the unsuspecting croupier, but undeterred she slid her King of Spades gently underneath her mystery card and flipped it into the air like an Olympic diver executing a simple rotation.

In super slow motion the dealer's card revealed itself next to the King.

Ace.

An Ace of fucking Spades.

Like watching passenger jets plow into the Twin Towers, I couldn't believe what I was seeing.

The God I didn't believe in had failed me.

"Blackjack," the dealer reluctantly called out.

A collective gasp from the audience broke the silence, simultaneously sucking the air from the room and my lungs.

The dealer funnelled my losing chips into a small black hole.

I wished I could have joined them.

My vision blurred and a huge wave of nausea swept over me like a giant vomit-y blanket.

I staggered from the table, my legs suddenly useless.

Was it possible to feel any worse than this?

HOW TO HIT ROCK BOTTOM

Deep in the bowels of a semi-detached house in the inner suburbs of Melbourne, Australia, I caught a glimpse of my future for the very first time.

It was a bleak destiny, one I neither planned for nor wanted.

A place so dark, that even fistfuls of ignited magnesium ribbon could not permeate its all-encompassing darkness.

There I was, gambling on a horse race in a country I was not in, using money I did not have, and knocking on a Pandora's box I never wanted to open.

I sat upright in my bed, laptop open, awash in a blue hue—something akin to the ultraviolet light bulbs installed in public toilets that prevent intravenous drug users from finding a vein.

All was not lost, however. I still had food in the pantry; so, if I blew the rent again, my major problems would not involve going hungry.

Speaking of food, the meal "toad in the hole" was a favorite dish. I couldn't help but chuckle at the irony after being forced to rename it "in the hole."

I had lost thousands of dollars doing this exact same thing

many nights before, but rather than dwell, I focused on my next major fix.

But I was not alone that night.

I had a great mate with me.

A friend that could persuade the unpersuadable,
would always say yes and never say no to some reckless, absurd,
and crazy adventure.
A friend that acted as my confidant, my worst enemy, and
everything in between.
I'd love for you to meet:
Alcohol.

Three bottles of appropriately priced pinot noir navigated its way through my veins. My poor liver bearing the brunt of it, now sluggish, fatty, and agitated at such abuse.

That warm, safe, and comfortable feeling that I had grown accustomed to when drunk, had long since disappeared into an anxious state of "fight or flight" driven by my skyrocketing cortisol levels.

"But red wine helps me relax."

Well, that's what I assumed, too.

"It helps me deal with the daily grind and repressed traumas; it frees me from the tyranny of reality… like socialising with friends and family members I tolerate, but can't actually stand."

Does it really?

For me, at a key crossroad in my life, I opted to squander money: rent money, food budgets, credit card advances, tax returns, and birthday cash from a great aunt I always promised to visit but never did.

Even if Bezos, Gates, and Musk had pooled their cash together to fund my degeneracy, it still would never have been enough, as it never filled that huge gaping hole of escapism.

In earlier times in my life, I had been virtuous—judging heroin addicts who sought so desperately their next hit.

But there I was, no better than them, except maybe for my living conditions.

Looking through my rose-colored glasses, everything on the surface was under control.

I was a tax paying citizen with plenty of great mates.

I held down great jobs, smashed sales targets, maintained wonderful relationships with my colleagues, and appeased and supported my manager.

I turned up on time, mostly kept my word and washed my bed sheets and pillowcases weekly.

I paid my bills, posted tailored birthday messages on the social media pages of my many, many friends, assisted grand-mothers across the road, carried their groceries—and on one special occasion, reinvigorated their lives (but more about that later).

But telling myself that I was in full control was about the biggest, fattest, ugliest fib I've ever told, and, boy, have I told a few.

Focusing my attention back towards my screen, I noticed a phone number in the bottom left-hand corner.

Why haven't I seen that before? I asked myself.

Further inspection revealed it to be the number for the gambler's helpline.

I read the number aloud slowly and raised my index finger like a golfer testing for wind speed.

I paused, then dialled.

Instinctively, I knew I needed more oxygen for what was about to transpire, so I sucked in a huge breath as if preparing to break a free-dive record.

The memory of doing something so scary, yet so empowering will never leave me.

That anxious, cortisol-y feeling was quickly replaced with adrenaline, hope, and excitement.

But mainly adrenaline.

Ring, Ring… Ring, Ring… Ring, Ring… the phone line clicked.

"Hello, this is Mary, your guardian angel, how may I protect you?"

Warm and silky like a chocolate fountain, Mary's voice cascaded down the line and enveloped my whole body.

Mary, yes, like *Mary Magdalene.*

She was my guardian angel whether she liked it or not.

A counselor for twenty years, Mary specialized in the

treatment of problem gambling.

And Mary, she had seen it all.

After probing me with some gentle open questions, I started to share everything, and the unloading began.

It had taken all my life to make this huge leap, and I'd be damned if I was leaving anything out. She listened with the patience of a saint, and my verbal diarrhea ended about the time poor Mary nearly broke.

When she had opportunity to respond, she spoke of the disproportionally high rates of suicide that problem gamblers experience.

According to the National Council on Problem Gambling, one in five pathological gamblers attempts suicide, a rate higher than for any other addictive disorder.

She went on to explain it's because gamblers lose everything so much more quickly, compared to other major addictive behaviors (such as drinking, drugs, porn, or sex).

That bone-jarring statistic shook me to my core.

I hadn't been that scared since I was a young lad watching Stephen King's terrifying horror flick *It*.

"Oh yes… they float, Georgie… they float… and when you're down here, with me… YOU'LL FLOAT, TOO!"

***

Growing up, being depressed, anxious, and vulnerable was

often associated with weakness.

It was uncomfortably glossed over like that inappropriate drunk boss we've all had, whose hands start wandering at the staff Christmas party.

We used to tolerate that back then; but, as with old "Handsy McGee", it's probably time we call out this very dangerous mental health elephant in the room.

This is especially important because in my own home country of New Zealand, the suicide rate for male youth in 2017 was the *third* highest across the Organization for Economic Cooperation and Development (OECD).

And female youth suicide rate was the highest![2]

We're talking about highly desired countries to live in here. That shows me we are not immune to this challenge anywhere in the world.

Mary's words made me ponder how many lives have ended long before their full potential was reached.

What impact on the world could those souls have had, if they allowed themselves to attain their dream life?

We'll likely never know the answer to that question until we can keep people around long enough to find out.

---

[2] Ministry of Health - Manatū Hauora, "An Overview of Suicide Statics," April 2017. www.health.govt.nz/system/files/documents/pages/data-story-overview-suicide-prevention-strategy-april2017newmap.pdf

Laban's random lessons:

Many people experience the same types of thoughts, fears, and worries I do/did:

1. Fear of judgement for admitting I have a problem (by calling the helpline and making it real).
2. Fear of shame for not being as tough as I thought I needed to be.
3. Fear of what my life would look like without (insert negative behavior here) in it.

The good news:

- Most of those fears never eventuated—and if they did, the impact was minor.
- The sheer relief outshone everything else, making fears a distant memory.

Think about it:

- What would your life look like with your demons under control?
- Who around you would that positively impact: your children, siblings, parents; hell, even your grandparents?
- Many times, people in our lives are just waiting for another person to make the first move.
- Maybe you should be the first person for once?
- Remember what Les Brown says, "Don't underestimate yourself. You are capable of more than you can ever imagine!"

THE DRAGON CHASER

The fascinating part of my own degenerate gambling habits: when I did win, I'd immediately increase the size of the next bet to try to achieve the same euphoria as before.

Recovered heroin addicts call this "chasing the dragon"... except in my case, my dragon was a purebred horse!

The first sliver of light entered my world after that first phone call with Mary.

Mary arranged for me to meet with a gambling psychologist and attend one-on-one sessions run by the Salvation Army.

It was free, professional therapy—and thank Christ for that, because I had less assets than post WW2 Germany.

Those sessions were funded by taxes collected from the gambling industry, so for the first time in my gambling career I actually ended up in the black.

Lee politely introduced herself, shook my hand, and sat down opposite me. She was a fully qualified, ridgy-didge, problem-gambler trainer-psychologist. Decades of taking on other people's problems were proudly exhibited across her deeply wrinkled forehead.

She had a natural warmth that made me trust her immediately, yet I felt tremendous guilt for placing another heavy burden across her brow. It became clear that Lee was living her purpose and the guilt soon passed.

These sessions were an opportunity for me to share for the first time in my life without judgement.

So, share, I did.

Lee started with one simple question about the relationship I had with my mum, and I immediately broke down.

Tears and guttural weeping erupted forth.

It's the kind of weeping you do when you're seventeen and in love for the first time, when your "forever" breaks it off without explanation and immediately starts dating someone else.

Or when your favorite grandparent dies and suddenly there are no more fishing trips.

This must have been pent up for a very long while as I felt immediate relief upon sharing.

Similar to the feeling Nelson Mandela had after being released from incarceration after twenty-seven long years.

I say similar because I wasn't there.

Now, I know what you're thinking, *Laban, you're comparing your emotional release to the plight of the twentieth century's greatest liberator of men, who was locked up for nearly three decades?*

Yes. Yes, I am.

Well, not exactly, but in terms of my twenty-seven years of metaphoric emotional jail time… you betcha!

Being trapped in emotional pain is a prison sentence for a crime you didn't know you committed and never realizing you've been locked up for it.

So, I chose to follow what Mandela did so beautifully: use a negative experience as my new advantage, a blessing in disguise if you will.

What I like to call the "Gift of Adversity."

The Gift of Adversity mindset allows us to take back our power by using the experience to our advantage and not wallowing in the victimhood of what happened to us.

We have very little actual control over what happens to us, but we absolutely have control over how we react to it.

Laban's random lessons:

Being in bondage to emotional pain was never a badge of honor.

When preparing to break free, it's good to find ideas and resources to help keep you sane. Read them; mull them over;

apply the principals at your own pace and in your own safe space. Here are a few that helped me:

- Treat yourself like someone you really care about.
- Lifelong repression of emotions causes a gradual loss of perspective. After years of dysfunction, my body adapted to the sustained pain and my brain eventually gave up and backed off. It allowed me to survive, but never thrive.
- Only time away from the pain allowed me to realize how destructive my feelings of defeat were. Relief offers a much-needed reference point.
- *Facing Codependence* by Pia Mellody was a brutally confronting book to read, but it probably saved my life. Special shout out to Timmy O'Toole for the recommendation.

That bit I said about having very little control over what happens to us, but we can control how we react? I'm not the only one that thinks that by the way.

Charles R. Swindoll, for example, once said, "Life is 10% what happens to you and 90% how you react."

Morgan Freeman + Mick Dundee

My mum and dad met in the summer of 1977.

Dad, a.k.a. Ric, was working as a fresh-faced "Midnight to Dawn" radio announcer; and Mum, a.k.a. Gail, was a talented hairdresser.

My father was a handsome man back in the day, but his amazing radio voice was the real panty-dropper.

Imagine a mix of Morgan Freeman and Crocodile Dundee. That was my dad!

They met after Mum rang up the radio station, slid her own sultry tongue through the phone receiver and requested "You Sexy Thing" by Hot Chocolate.

Mum was a red-headed stunner but easily fell into the "Danger Zone" on the *Crazy/Hot Matrix*. My father, oblivious to the impending danger and led only by his testosterone, was no match.

The two struck up an intense romance and within three short months, Dad had moved out of his shoebox into Mum's house.

She carried a young son from her first marriage—my older half-brother, which is probably an important point to mention.

Mum and Dad were together six years before the chocolaty goodness turned bitter enough for them to do something about it and they finally parted ways when I was three years old.

Most couples that break up pray for a civil split or conscious uncoupling; unfortunately, on this occasion, it became a bloodied disembowelment!

But these were just two people who were doing the best they could with the tools they had available at the time.

It wasn't enough to keep them together, however.

My father eventually found solace in the arms of his blond-haired personal secretary.

Insert penis and cliché here.

Dad's mistress was three months pregnant when he moved out for the final time.

Talk about making your life complicated.

After my first few sessions with Lee, the psychologist, I began to comprehend that what I experienced growing up, while prolific in society, wasn't normal, let alone functional.

Society still does not completely understand the impact divorce has on children; but we do know it often leaves a trail of devastation one way or another.

The day my parents split is one I remember well, even though for most of my life I struggled to recall anything from my infancy through my late teens.

Modern psychology attributes memory loss to a coping mechanism our very clever brains utilize.

Repressing memories might seem like a good idea at the time, but I'm still a much bigger fan of "better out than in."

A child's brain doesn't have the same extent of wiring that a fully developed adult brain has, so children will repress memories in lieu of having a full-blown mental breakdown if the trauma is too much.

Not surprisingly, children's brains are ill-equipped to handle the same battering that our grown-up brains can.

My youngest brother has no recollection of the split (perhaps given his age), but my older half-brother, who was ten years old at the time, does.

No stranger to this situation, he was about to experience his second lot of abandonment in only a few short years.

Mum's first husband, and his biological father, abandoned him at a very young age. The effect on any child is brutal once, let alone twice.

During Dad's final day with us, he and my Mum were conferenced in their bedroom for what felt like an eternity.

Their voices were muffled by inches of plasterboard and funky 1970s wallpaper, but it was very apparent this was no UN-led peace talk.

The house vibrated with super low waves of negative energy. You could almost taste the impending doom with a modicum of intuition.

But their furious negotiations eventually petered out, finishing with an eerie moment of silence before my father's bedraggled body appeared from around the corner.

I jumped to attention and stood steadfast in front of my dad just like Tank Man did in Tiananmen Square.

And just like Tank Man, I wasn't going anywhere.

Dad looked over at me and his eyes lit up momentarily. Despite an ambitious smile, you could clearly see that he was desperately protecting a broken soul.

Before I could say anything, he scooped me up, wrapped both arms around me, and whispered, "Daddy has to go now."

His Magnum PI-inspired moustache tickled my face. With a kiss on my flushed cheek, he was gone.

Due to the laws around divorce in New Zealand in the early 1980s, the mother was almost always given the majority of custody, while the father was made out to be a pariah (whether deserved or not). Fortnightly weekend visits were the only penance for a "lucky" father.

An invisible punishment for allowing the family to be broken apart, perhaps.

Having had the benefit of many years to reflect, I now get the reasons why my parents chose to split—and, in many ways, I'm thankful that they did.

I've spoken to countless individuals who were children of loveless marriages (including my own father) and 100% of the outcomes have been devastating to the children in one way, shape, or another.

Studies repeatedly show that marriages that stay together on the whole, are much better for everyone involved long-term. Although I think we all know some relationships that would've concluded with an OJ and Nicole Simpson style ending if not for the option of divorce.

I can only imagine how miserable it must be for parents who chose to ignore the signals and stay locked together, fearful of what the kids will say or do if they end the marriage. Most kids seem far more understanding than parents give them credit for.

***

For years I held onto the burning embers of resentment for "what my parents did to me." But my mindset began to change when I understood an important fact: it's up to me to move forward. Once I took total ownership of my life, I began to lead from the front, setting new standards of self-care, self-love, and self-generosity.

I'm pleased to report that after counseling (and massive improvements in my overall nutrition, health, and well-being) many of my childhood memories have returned.

I've also learned to take full advantage of the powerful medium that is the internet, to effectively be the change I want to see (with some extra help).

I highly recommend it.

We live in an age where a few keystrokes can change a life—your life, more importantly.

Our parents, depending on their age, didn't have the same access to information that we have now.

Once you are empowered with new knowledge, you'll set yourself on your own journey of healing and leadership, so that when you become responsible for other human beings (as a parent, guardian, mentor, or whatever), you'll have the tools to impart positivity and functional behaviour to the next generation.

Personally, I have been able to repair the majority of my life with information gleaned off the internet. I even found a recipe for chicken liver pâté that makes your spine tingle. Love or hate it, it's a powerful resource—and one for which I am eternally grateful.

John Lennon died in 1980, but many years later his words still resonate with me.

[Read aloud in your best Beatles accent for maximum effect]

"There are two basic motivating forces: fear and love. When we are afraid, we pull back from life. When we are in love, we open to all that life has to offer with passion, excitement, and acceptance. We need to learn to love ourselves first, in all our glory and our imperfections. If we cannot love

ourselves, we cannot fully open to our ability to love others or our potential to create. Evolution and all hopes for a better world rest in the fearlessness and open-hearted vision of people who embrace life."

Laban's random lessons:

Parents, for the most part, are just grown-up children. They are a direct reflection of their own upbringing and environment. We need to be gentler in our judgement sometimes.

The best suggestion I can offer to children of dysfunctional parents: focus on self-development with the goal of breaking the cycle of dysfunction and trauma in yourself.

Forgiving ourselves (and then everyone else) is such an effective pathway that it should be added to every school's curriculum immediately.

If you ever experience a trigger for any repressed memory, be kind to yourself and seek the guidance of a trained professional. A good professional can empower you with much needed confidence and allow a far smoother healing journey than trying to figure it out on your own.

It might take you a few attempts; but keep trying until you find someone that you really connect with.

You'll know when you do and if it's all too hard, you're probably heading in the wrong direction.

As Nelson Mandela once said, "One of the things I learned when I was negotiating was that until I changed myself, I could not change others."

GENEROSITY

Friday, June 27, 1986, was my sixth birthday and the last day of the school week.

The last period of the day was sport and we often played a game called scrag.

The only description of scrag that I can make would be a full body-contact game that combines rugby without a ball and prison rioting without a knife. It has also, I might add, been banned across school yards due to excessive broken bones and bruised organs (but mainly due to an overwhelming groundswell of snowflake, helicopter parents).

I made it through the battle unscathed on that particular day. Maybe because all the other kids knew it was my special day and wanted to keep me "pretty" for my celebratory birthday photograph.

They need not have worried. There would be no paparazzi shoot happening that night.

Mum had made the God inspired decision to send her two sons to a privately run Christian school on a social welfare allowance. And money was tighter than a duck's butt.

By quick estimate, the actual dollar amount Mum received

from the government was probably close to the amount of our school fees.

But I've gotta give her credit. She somehow managed two years of high-quality education on the smell of an oily rag, though that rag was constantly running out of fumes.

I was a passenger in her Ford Cortina station wagon on more occasions than I care to remember, being asked to pray to God so that we would have enough gas to make it home. Sometimes he answered, more often he didn't.

It's only in the last few years that I've even allowed my own car gas tank to get anywhere near halfway. An enduring legacy of trudging my way to the gas station to borrow a jerry can and a few bucks worth of juice to get us home. Character building stuff, I assure you.

Most kids at my school had parents who bought them McDonald's at lunchtime, fish and chips on Friday, and gave them Coco Pops for breakfast. *Those bastards!*

I'm grateful for not eating that garbage now, but I wasn't then.

I was fed a monotonous schedule of Vegemite sandwiches, occasional fruit, and on rare occasions, a chocolate chip muesli bar or two.

But if you combine the energy I expended from simply growing, plus the energy demands from the exercise I was doing, the calories I was allocated were simply not enough.

Riding my bike to school, alone, burned so much fuel.

Aww, that's cute... you rode your bike to school?

Well, if by "rode" you mean competed in an unofficial Tour de France, then yes.

I've researched the exact distance using mapping software, and my still-to-this-day defined calf muscles proudly display the efforts of riding 18 km a day (that's a little over eleven miles for those of you holding out on the proper measurement scale).

Yes, that's 9 km (over five and a half miles) each way—at five years old.

Surely that's equivalent to an Ironman triathlon (at least the cycle bit).

Five years of age, trailing behind my thirteen-year-old brother, navigating the perpendicular streets of Christchurch with my orange Stack hat on. Sure, I was chaperoned by my brother, but my little legs were still doing all the pumping, and if you tried to get *your child* to do the same in this day and age, you'd be jailed immediately and left there to rot!

I'd often arrive home from school famished and there wouldn't be a lot to eat despite Mum's grand efforts.

Many times, the only sustenance would be foil wrapped stock cubes which, when mixed with hot water, congealed into an Oliver Twist gruel-like substance.

If you're unsure what I'm talking about, here's the ingredients list:

Wheat Flour (with added Calcium, Iron, Niacin & Thiamine), Salt, Dried Glucose Syrup, Monosodium Glutamate,

Chicken Fat, Potato Starch, Sugar, Concentrated Chicken Extract, and Ammonia Caramel to give it that real natural look.

I wouldn't feed that chemical warfare to my worst enemy these days, however back then with my North Korean levels of starvation, it tasted just like nectar of the gods.

Back to our game, it had just finished, and I was standing in an orderly queue of young men who were waiting on one of the teachers to re-tie our school ties.

It was a proper tie—not one of those handy ties with an elastic band that you could snap on in only a few short seconds.

But I ask you, how many five years olds do you know that can form a Windsor knot? (K)not many!

My uniform was an oversized green blazer, purchased three sizes too big, so I could grow into it.

It consumed my charcoal black shorts (also too big) and covered up the standard white buttoned shirt with long sleeves.

Every Friday we'd stand in that line and allow an exceptionally talented teacher to whip that unnecessary fashion accessory into a work of art.

That week it was Mrs. Amanda Neil, a substitute teacher filling in for our usual teacher, Mrs. Bucknell, who was gallivanting across Europe.

Mrs. Neil kept our class up to date with Mrs. Bucknell's travels by placing pins with string on them on a world map to show the latest destination at which the teacher had arrived. Pretty much the next best thing to Google maps back then.

Whilst Mrs. Bucknell was away, we were asked to write and send postcards throughout her trip. One of mine read, "I hope it's not too slippery in Greece."

I was basically a comedic genius at six years of age, but never formally recognized.

"What are you doing this weekend?" Mrs. Neil asked the boy at the front of the queue.

"We're going skiing at Mount Hutt!" the lad replied excitedly.

"Wow, that's great. You be sure to look after yourself up there," Mrs. Neil affectionately replied.

The skier disappeared and the teacher asked the same question to the kid in front of me. He responded with something equally exciting. His tie was done and off he went.

I approached Mrs. Neil with a slight apprehension, as I knew the question was coming, and I didn't feel like answering it truthfully.

I had always been an outwardly happy child despite the obvious challenges, but it was hard to brave-face it on such a momentous occasion.

The question came quicker than I expected and caught me off guard.

"What are you doing this weekend, Laban?" she asked softly.

"It's my birthday!" I blurted out, never one to hide the great moments in life.

"Happy birthday, Laban! What a wonderful day it is; what are you doing to celebrate?"

There it was. She got me.

I had no option but to spill the beans.

"Umm," I stammered. "Nothing Miss… Mum said we don't have any money at the moment, but she'll make it up to me as soon as she can."

I smiled bravely.

Mrs. Neil's warm disposition morphed into an "I've-just-witnessed-a-small-puppy-get-run-over-by-a-car" look. It was quite remarkable to watch.

"Oh," she replied, clearly not expecting that response.

She composed herself and in a soft, quivery voice said, "I'm sorry to hear that Laban. I'm sure your birthday will still be fantastic."

I could see a rogue tear leave her left eye and run part way down her cheek before she captured it under the guise of a pretend swatting of a bug to the face.

She finished sorting my tie in silence and then sent me on my way.

The school bell rang, and we all started dispersing out to take our respective routes home.

I took my orange Stack hat and made my way to the bike sheds.

As I grabbed my miniature BMX by the handlebars, Mrs. Neil appeared.

She had many more tears in her eyes and from nowhere, thrust a plain envelope into my palm.

She issued me stern instructions, like that of a WW2 lieutenant ordering a platoon of troops to make a pivotal strike that will change the outcome of the war.

"Laban, do not open this. Take this straight home and give it to your mother."

When you're that young, you do what you're told… so, I did.

Setting a new land speed record getting home, I flew up the driveway and nearly bowled over Rusty, the family King Charles cocker spaniel.

Dumping my bike on the front porch, I ran into the house, and passed the contraband to Mum.

"What's this?" she asked.

I repeated Mrs. Neil's instructions, as Mum slowly opened the envelope.

I tried to speed up the process by telekinesis—thinking *hurry up*—the same way we do when waiting for really slow people on an escalator.

I heard a sharp gasp from my mother's mouth, followed by a loud, high-pitched, "Oh my God, it's a miracle."

Mum revealed the contents in the same way Rafiki, the shaman baboon, reveals Simba, the Lion King, to the world.

Mrs. Amanda Neil had enclosed thirty beautiful dollars into that envelope—10% of a relief-teacher's net weekly wage in those days.

Hakuna Matata! It meant no worries for the rest of that day at least.

Unbeknownst to Mrs. Neil at the time, she single-handedly changed the course of my life in the process.

This single act of generosity not only funded one of the greatest impromptu birthday parties on record, but (more importantly) allowed an impressionable young man to witness first-hand a truly selfless act of generosity. It has stayed with me to this day and has influenced many of my own acts of giving.

***

Despite the vivid memory of the event, no one could actually recall the teacher's name. After word got out that this book was being written, a manhunt was launched at Middleton Grange School in Christchurch, New Zealand, and Mrs. Amanda Neil was eventually tracked down and contact made, thirty-four long years in the making.

When I re-shared this story with Amanda, her response was truly humbling.

Being acknowledged so long after the event was almost too much for her to handle; but handle it she did.

The joy I experienced reliving that moment with her was

worth the effort of writing the book alone.

In return, I now receive tailored digital e-cards from Amanda every Christmas, birthday, and Easter.

We have spent many hours on the phone together talking about all manner of life's interesting twists and turns. For example, she left a career in teaching to become a priest, dedicating her life once again to service.

Laban's random lessons:

Giving can almost seem selfish at times, as the response from the universe seems to magnify our generosity back in ways far greater than I yet fully understand.

It's good to try the theory out for yourself on a regular basis:

Practice at least one daily act of giving, to anybody you choose—the teenage worker at the supermarket, the person at the car wash, the postie or the IT support guy located thousands of miles away.

Do this with zero expectation of anything in return and repeat the process as often as possible.

It can be as simple as a smile or authentic interest in someone's day.

For example, when someone says hello and asks how you are, respond with, "Do you know what… I'm truly blessed."

Ninety-nine out of 100 times it will start a conversation that will change your whole day for the better (and theirs)!

Receiving an honest compliment might be the only positive experience in someone's entire day.

And it just might have a positive impact on your own life, in ways you never imagined.

In the words of Zig Ziglar, "You can have everything in life you want, if you will just help enough other people get what they want."

THE COCAINE OLYMPICS

After six months with the psychologist, I had started to make solid improvements, but I was still very much a work in progress.

However, I was starring in my first television-style acting role, and my spirits were high.

I was the lead actor in a commercial for an anti-violence initiative.

The organization, *Step Back Think*, was created after a local Melbourne boy, James Macready-Bryan was left with permanent brain damage after a stranger attacked him without provocation on his twentieth birthday.

The goal of the organization was aimed at the prevention of what's commonly known as a "king hit." It involves punching someone in the head, usually from behind and knocking the victim unconscious. Most of the damage is done when they slump unconscious at speed and hit the concrete awkwardly. It has since been more accurately rebranded as a "coward punch."

Not only was the opportunity to play the lead part exciting and positive for me, but it was also for a great cause.

Alongside the excitement of my newfound fame, I had

been invited to a friend's birthday party in the city.

I rushed straight from work and neglected to put any food in my stomach.

With a large bar tab on offer, I launched straight into the hard liquor. Within sixty minutes, I had easily drunk enough for two people; I should have called it a night and been happy with that.

But, for the millionth time in my life, I would rather die than go home early and miss out on all the fun.

I was drunk enough to know that I needed at least one of two things.

A.   Something starch-y, or
B.   Something cocaine-y

I got wind that someone had *Bolivian Marching Powder* and within minutes I had quite literally sniffed them out.

Grabbing the miniature Ziploc bag, I darted into the men's bathroom and locked myself away in an imaginary fortress.

Plunging a makeshift spoon (my house key) into the bag, I wiggled it around, and heaped as large an amount as was physically possible onto it.

With the precision of an eye surgeon, I withdrew the key perfectly from the bag, and proceeded to jam the entire contents into my left nostril.

My spare pinky finger held the right nostril closed as I

snorted as hard as my lungs would allow—inhaling with such gusto, the embossed *Yale* imprint on the key nearly lifted out.

As the powder made its way deep into my nasal cavity, I repeated the process with my opposite nostril and allowed the drug to take effect.

If you've never taken cocaine, the closest I can describe my own experience is that feeling you get when you see yourself on the television—you know, in the background during a news report or three seconds of your opinion piece… when you told everyone you know to tune in to channel seven, so they could watch you in action.

It's a nearly instantaneous euphoria, followed by a sharp, miniature panic attack.

Your heart beats so fast that Greta Thunberg appears out of nowhere and starts charging her pink Tesla Model 3 from your fingertips.

I can't tell you how many times I have blatantly ignored serious health symptoms that would hospitalize most people, whilst ingesting drugs. That's why I rarely did cocaine by itself as I needed the numbing effect of alcohol to level me out a little.

As the devil's dandruff absorbed into my bloodstream, I immediately snapped out of my drunken stupor, and transformed into an articulate, witty, hilarious, and debonair young man.

I checked my nose for residue, swaggered out of the bathroom, and headed back towards my pals.

If you've ever observed any flagrant drug use, you'll likely identify with this story with an agreeable nod. People taking drugs in toilets these days are about as subtle as an axe.

That articulate, witty, hilarious, and debonair young man I described was far from any of those characteristics.

Yes, your ability to tolerate alcohol improves, but if you go too far, the wheels spin off in all directions.

Thump! I felt a firm hand grab my shoulder, and I spun around expecting to see one of my hilarious friends.

"I'm sorry sir, but you have to leave," bellowed the six-foot-eight giant of a man.

"And for what reason?" I belligerently spat. Several droplets of my own saliva projecting onto his barrel chest.

"You've had too much to drink, and you have to leave."

"That's horseshit!" I said. "I'm perfectly fine."

No sooner had I declared my sobriety, then I removed my favorite blue t-shirt in protest.

I started swinging it around my head like a deranged Greenpeace activist.

"Right. You're outta here, punk."

Resistance was futile, so I headed towards the exit stairs that led out to the main street.

As I reached the bottom of the stairs, the bouncer bid me farewell with a rather loud, "Get the fuck out of here!"

Now, I may have been intoxicated, breaking all the rules

and high on illegal substances, but I certainly wouldn't be spoken to like that.

"You get the fuck outta here!"

NOTE: There are no random lessons here, other than cocaine makes you a dick. If you're using it, then you might want to quit lest you outdick me.

POLICE COPS

Let's start this chapter where we left off. Let's tease out this disastrous evening a little more.

Six uniformed police officers standing around the main entrance of the bar all turned and looked at me.

"Oi, you just watch your language, son!" one of the cops yelled back at me.

The reptilian part of my brain took over just long enough for me to do something real silly.

"Oh yeah? Go fuck yourself!" I screamed back.

Momentarily catching them off guard with my outrageous proclamation, their years of training kicked in and I immediately sensed trouble.

One officer lurched toward me as I spun on my heels and Usain Bolted off in the opposite direction.

Stunned passers-by soon realized they were witnessing a real-life police chase; rather than try to subdue me, they yelled encouragement, whooping and yahooing their speedy protagonist.

I could hear police footsteps pounding behind me, but I dropped the hammer and gave it all I had.

Despite my portly figure, I was fast once I was up and going.

The footsteps trailed off and faded away into nothing.

Had I achieved Shawshank Redemption with an Andy Dufresne style of freedom?

Plus, isn't escaping from a police pursuit a bucket list event for everyone? Tick ✓

I'd travelled well over four hundred yards at that point, not even the world's fittest runners could sustain the pace I was setting, especially when plied with drugs and alcohol.

The footpath on which I ran was part of a larger arcade where the main tram system runs down the middle.

This, as it turns out, was a fantastic location for police cars to drive down.

To my horror, four patrol cars sped past me in the section where the trams would usually be, and I knew at that point I was running out of options.

Using all my cunning, I noticed a dark alleyway on the opposite side. I doubled back across the tram lines and headed towards the fantastic hiding spot.

Nuzzling into that amazingly discreet cubby hole, I shrunk into the smallest ball of a human I could contort.

Up to that point, I thought I had escaped scot-free—then I heard the deafeningly loud police megaphone burst into life.

"Freeze! Come out with your hands where I can see them!"

Perhaps they're yelling at someone else, I thought optimistically.

"You, with the blue t-shirt."

OK, that narrowed it down. The numbers were certainly stacked against *me*. It probably was me they were after.

"YOU, come out NOW!"

The shape of a police-issued handgun is a very distinctive one and the sight of one being pointed at your face evokes a few different emotions.

Like the popular, *"Do what you are told, Ditchburn"* emotion.

Equally, having a gun pointed at your face also triggers the rapid tightening of the sphincter muscle.

Had I not gone earlier that night, I suspect I would have been arrested for at least one count of soiling my pants.

So, like a tulip opening in the springtime, I slowly unfolded out of my cocoon and revealed myself to the world.

Boom! I was tackled from behind and before I even knew what was happening, I was face down with my wrists firmly secured in handcuffs behind my back.

I channelled a lifetime of television memories in a vain attempt to remember how to break out of handcuffs.

Nope. Nothing.

It required two items I didn't have anyway: a hairclip and shoulder flexibility.

Sometimes in life, you just know when to call it quits.

I haven't felt many moments of helplessness in my life,

but that was one.

It must've been a slow night, because I was eventually surrounded by what felt like every police officer in Melbourne.

It was like that final scene out of the *The Blues Brothers* movie when Jake and Elwood pay the $5,000 to City Hall and then find themselves with a peacock's tail of guns pointing at them.

Always the comedian, I politely asked the cop, "What seems to be the problem, officer?"

The guns were away at this point, so my chances of being shot in the face had dramatically reduced.

Someone fitting my description had coward punched someone right near where I launched my escape, and I was the main suspect.

Mind you, in 2015 "bald and with a beard" described every thirty-five-year-old male in Australia.

I chuckled to myself at the irony of what had just happened.

The cop asked me what was so funny.

I carefully explained that I was the lead actor in a very important anti-coward punch campaign.

The look on his face was one of pure disbelief. Even I will admit it sounds unbelievable, but whilst they were checking for outstanding arrest warrants, one of the cops pulled out his phone to call my bluff on the video.

Two of them watched my artistic genius whilst I remained on my knees, then they both turned their attention to their walkie talkies.

Headquarters had radioed through that the actual violent perpetrator had been picked up at another nearby location, so my alibi stood firm.

I avoided being arrested that night by the bee's dick and I'm super appreciative that they didn't press charges, even if it was under "wasting police time."

In terms of stupidity, that's right up there.

And not just the risky situation. I found out later that the nightclub I was at, is directly opposite one of the largest police stations in Victoria. *Facepalm*

I called it a night and made my way home sheepishly. I crawled into bed and drifted slowly off to sleep, lingering traces of adrenaline causing my eyes to occasionally flick open.

The following morning, the sun lightsabered its way into my room, and a disturbing pounding noise emanated from the house.

I craned my neck around but couldn't see anything obvious.

It didn't take long to realize that the rather large beating drum was actually in my head.

Boom... boom... boom... BOOM!

Just like the Vengaboys used to sing.

My brain quickly scanned for all possible medical issues.

Diagnosis: a grade five hangover.

I had managed one many times before and knew how to handle it.

The associated grogginess would eventually dissipate, but what I didn't account for was the huge waves of anxiety that swept over me.

Broken memories from the previous night came flooding back and I cringed regretfully at my behaviour.

I was, for all intents and purposes, a well-adjusted human being, yet I had just acted like Alex DeLarge from *A Clockwork Orange*.

This was a pivotal moment in my life. I had cut it way too close to the danger zone; I was riding Lady Luck just a little too hard.

Laban's random lessons:

I'm not saying don't have fun, but before things get out of hand, ask yourself:

- If I was on the receiving end of this behaviour, how would I feel?

- And if I'm not the one doing it, am I encouraging it by saying nothing?

Since making a much more concerted effort to surround myself with higher quality people, these types of behaviours are no longer acceptable to me.

> *"The right thing to do and the hard thing*
> *to do are usually the same."*
> —Steve Maraboli, *Life, the Truth, and Being Free*

HONG KONG PHOOEY

In 2015, during a planned vacation across China, I performed what must be known as one of the most outrageous acts of infidelity ever committed.

I was in a Tinder-inspired relationship that was nearing twelve months and had been rocky for quite some time.

She and I shared a deeply dysfunctional relationship that was made worse by alcohol-fueled fights that would make Ike and Tina Turner blush.

No physical exchanges ever took place but as we all know, the tongue can often inflict just as much damage as a fist. One example argument started over something I'll never remember, but ended with me demanding that we play a super-aggressive game of "Marry, Fuck, Kill."

If you've never played, it involves being given three different (usually famous) people.

Of those three, you must then choose which one you would marry, fuck, and kill.

Totally fictional, of course, and usually played with great humor and spirit, except on that particular occasion when I was filthy angry at her and out for maximum hurt.

I carefully choose my three options.

My belligerent and red wine-stained mouth yelling at the top of my voice and proudly declaring that I would…

Marry Satan!

Fuck Hitler!

Kill her!

I know, I know, *I know*… it's outrageous and totally inappropriate but, hey, it happened so what am I gonna do, right?

Her look of confusion, disbelief, and then blind rage reminded me of that Michael Jackson video clip "Black or White" when the people's faces morph into the next person's. Except these faces weren't happy ones!

By some miracle of Christ, we patched things up enough to go on our holiday together.

A five-city trip that started in Shanghai, meandered through Beijing, Chongqing, and Shenzhen, and ended in Hong Kong.

I stuck one up the Chinese Communist party by "checking in" on the Great Wall using a banned Facebook app. *You rebel, Laban!*

Our time together was civil enough; we even managed a few decent moments together.

There were four days of my explosive stomach flu that my ex had to contend with, so I suppose the only way to repay her generosity was to cheat on her.

With the gastro in full remission, we were on our final

leg of the trip in Hong Kong, staying with a good friend of mine who lived there. He kindly offered up his bedroom and arranged a final day "junket" or junk for short.

A junk is a boat that is loaded with food, booze, and music and you enjoy the freedom that being on the water provides whilst taking on as much free alcohol as possible.

Any responsible service of alcohol goes out the window and plenty of yahooing and frivolity is had by all. A rabble of us enjoyed the festivities and we made the most of the short time we still had in Hong Kong.

The junk ended at sunset, and we all left to go back to our host's place to continue the party.

Throughout the entire China trip, during moments of weakness and general curiosity, I had intermittently down-loaded the popular dating app, Tinder.

I'm not sure what I was looking for specifically, but it was probably attention more than anything.

There were plenty of seemingly lonely women that worked and lived all across China who were seeking interactions with a "nice guy." And as a "single" Anglo-Saxon man, I was somewhat of a rarity, it seemed, for I had no trouble matching online with those who reciprocated.

I excused myself from the main party and slinked off to the bathroom. In my drunken state, I sat down to pee; using this sit down position to my advantage, I began to swipe right (on the app, not my bum) and was immediately matched with an attractive lass.

A few risqué messages were sent to test the waters, as there was no point beating around the bush with the time constraints in place. We were flying back to Australia the next morning on a red eye and time was of the essence.

The Tinderella was English but worked in Hong Kong as a time-poor executive. She was obviously more open-minded than I realized.

I'm still astounded at how quick it all happened. Within minutes, a few cheeky messages had turned into an invite to her place for a "night-cap."

To enhance my credibility further, I told the mystery woman I was a professional voice-over artist who had a flight to Spain (muchas gracias)in four hours to record a really important television commercial. That helped explain why I couldn't stay long. She was totally fine with that, and *¡No podía creer mi suerte!* (I couldn't believe my luck!)

My real partner was tired from the day's events and had gone to bed to sleep it off. The flight back to Melbourne was super early, so she had made me promise I wouldn't be too much longer. "Of course," I solemnly swore.

I tiptoed into the bedroom to grab my wallet, a fresh shirt, and a few pumps of aftershave (bought for me by my girlfriend!).

I told my mate that I was heading downstairs to get some more lemonade and ice for our vodka. He was caught up in his own dance party and just nodded in approval.

Hailing a taxi, I showed the cab driver the address. We pulled up to the apartment complex in less than ten minutes and I quickly realized the enormity of the situation.

I'm on holiday with my girlfriend, in a foreign country, trying to repair what's left of our relationship, and I'm about to booty-call some random lass on a dating app.

Oh my God, you horrible bastard, I thought, smiling to myself—then proceeded to ring the doorbell.

My self-loathing never really stopped me from self-destructive behaviour before, so why should it start?

In the interest of keeping this PG, a few drinks were had to acquaint ourselves and then the deed was done.

A quick shower at my lover's house, and before I knew it, I was back in a taxi on my way back to my mate's house and my sleeping girlfriend.

At least, that's what I thought she was doing.

I arrived home to find the party over, so I slinked back into the bedroom, hoping not to awaken my sleeping beauty.

I need not have worried as my "sleeping beauty" was bolt upright in bed and more awake than ever.

"Where the HELL have you been?!" she demanded.

I had been gone for over two hours at that point.

The local shop was less than a minute's walk away from the apartment, so I had about 118 minutes of lost time to account for.

"Oh, hey, babe," I said, downplaying the situation, "I got to chatting with some crazy Irish guys and the time got carried away."

Lying must release its own vibrational frequency because she could sense it a mile away. She wasn't buying it for a second.

"Why did you put on aftershave and change your shirt?!"

"I was smelly?" I asked the question for both of us, my voice inflecting upwards, thus indicating bullshit.

"YOU'VE been at a brothel, haven't you?!" She screamed.

Now, the good news was that I had not been at a brothel, so with all the conviction of a Bill Clinton impeachment hearing, I stood there with my hand on my heart and declared to her the following.

"I did not have sexual relations with a prostitute at that brothel."

Damn you're good, I arrogantly thought to myself, drifting off and imagining an Academy Award for my "once in a generation" performance.

In reality this situation was more like a "Razzie", the award for the worst film of the year.

Obviously devastated, she conceded and rolled over, pretending to go back to sleep.

A pounding headache and an ice-cold death stare is a terrible way to wake up. Our taxi ride to the airport was equally frosty.

As soon as we arrived, she went her separate way and

rebooked our seating so that we were as far apart as physically possible.

Not surprisingly, we broke up within days of arriving back.

She believed and accepted my terrible lie about the Irish lads, and was keen to try and repair things, but I called it off as it was clear by now that I had zero respect for myself, let alone her. She didn't deserve to be treated like that so ending it was the best option in my humble opinion.

And just in case my ex-girlfriend happens to learn the actual truth via reading this:

I am truly sorry for my behavior and I hope you can forgive me.

I'll strategically leave this here.

Helpful reading: *Forgive for Good: A Proven Prescription for Health and Happiness* by Dr. Fred Luskin

THE ANGEL OF DEATH

For a not-quite-three-year-old, I was a cheeky little bugger and incredibly mobile.

We lived two doors down from the local dairy, milk-bar, or corner store (depending on what part of the world you are in) and I would often steal coins from my mother's milk-money jar and tootle up the road where they would sell me an assortment of cheap candies.

Smokers, milk bottles, aniseed drops, Eskimos (now renamed Inuit due to racist connotations), and *coke bottles* (a jelly substance that tasted like cola, but contained no cola).

The shopkeeper knew my parents well but incorrectly assumed it was perfectly acceptable to sell me these diabolical treats. Christ only knows the impact on a toddler who consumes all that sugar, but that's easily another story/lawsuit all together.

It's not like Mum and Dad encouraged this behavior.

They locked me in behind a gate that separated the street from our driveway. About six feet tall and made of treated wood panels, its horizontal stabilizing beam made a great platform to climb over.

The argument around whether we evolved from monkeys is still hotly contested, but if you'd seen the way in which I ascended that fence, you'd be well within your rights to clasp your hands together and proudly proclaim, "Well, that settles it, we came from monkeys!"

I would scale that thing with Spiderman-like agility, leveraging myself over the top to drop down six feet onto the grass verge below.

If attempted by a mature adult, both kneecaps would explode out the front of their legs like a scene from *Saving Private Ryan*.

But off I'd go, knees intact, and within seconds, I'd literally become a kid in a candy store.

On one special mission, I fell awkwardly when dismounting on the other side of the fence and banged my head.

My distraught mother came and rescued me, dusted me off, and sent me to bed to sleep it off.

I woke the next day displaying flu-like symptoms. I had a raised temperature and didn't enjoy being exposed to light very much.

Dad was away for business at the time. So, Mum took me down to the local GP where I was quickly diagnosed with a fever, given some paracetamol, and told to go home.

Doctor knows best, so Mum brought me home and again sent me to bed.

Over the next five days my condition deteriorated dramatically.

My eyes involuntarily rolled back into my head, my neck stiffened and contorted in an awkward and painful manner, and that sensitivity to light became intolerable.

Mum had called the doctor's office again and was told the same thing. *It's probably a fever. Just give it a few days to sort it out.*

I was inconsolable and Mum was at her wits' end. She called my father, relayed the symptoms to him and he immediately jumped on the next plane back home.

I was taken to the emergency department of Canterbury's premier hospital located in the heart of Christchurch.

It was an amazing facility with state-of-the-art equipment—the best of breed available in the South Island of New Zealand at the time.

At that stage, I had been displaying severe symptoms for five days straight.

Any parent this day and age would be able to jump online and within seconds, work out that their child was minutes from death or easily conclude that what their child actually had was harmless.

It's usually the former based on my experience.

More than two hours passed, and we were still waiting to be seen by the doctor. My temperature was sky high and my photosensitivity so acute that my eyes needed a spare jumper to block out all the light.

An orderly happened to walk past where Mum, Dad, and I were waiting. He caught a quick glimpse of me and without taking the time to introduce himself, demanded loudly, "How long has that child been like that?"

Mum looked up, seeking any solace at this point, and replied desperately, "My son has been like this for five days."

The orderly looked her in the eye and said in a firm but caring manner, "Wait here; do not go anywhere."

When you're that frightened, you tend to do what you are told, so she did. The orderly then disappeared into the bowels of the red and white painted emergency surgery area.

A voice boomed over the intercom and reverberated down the corridors, "Code Blue, ER, Code Blue, ER."

I was rushed into the operating room and immediately administered a five-inch lumbar-puncture plunged straight into my backbone, without anaesthetic. The excuse being there was not enough time to give me the pain relief usually received.

My blood curdling screams ricocheted across the entire length of the hospital ward—to this day, the thought still sends shivers down the spines of both my parents. Which is ironic because that is where they stick you with the needle!

The results of the spinal tap revealed some serious shit. Advanced bacterial meningitis.

Bacterial meningitis being the most serious type of meningitis.

It can lead to death or permanent disability within hours.

Meningitis affects the meninges, the membranes that surround the brain and spinal cord and protect the central nervous system, together with the cerebrospinal fluid.

The doctor explained that the bump on my head from my fall likely allowed a vulnerability in my immune system for the bacteria to flourish.

My condition was severe, and everyone knew it.

My father grabbed the doctor by his white coat sleeve and desperately demanded to know when I would be OK to come home.

"Mr. Ditchburn," he yelled. "I can't guarantee your child will live through the night."

Blindsided by the news, my father panicked and started wailing, "He's going to end up maimed or brain-damaged, I just know it!"

My mother had other ideas and thumped her fists into my father's chest and yelled back at him with all her lung power, "Our son is going to live!" She insisted.

In my life, I have witnessed enough amazing events to know that someone is looking after me. I'm sure you have the same when you really think about it.

My devoutly religious mother rallied her local church to arrange a candlelight vigil. Even non-believers started praying to Allah, Buddha, and Jesus in the faint hope that maybe, just maybe, one of them might help.

My Nana, Andrea Henderson, who was easily an angel on Earth but hardly ultra-religious, had her own "God moment;" she spoke of a vision of me being lifted up and surrounded by angels, who gently reassured her that I was going to be fine.

Thank you, Nana, I appreciate that tremendously.

Within hardly any time at all, and by the grace of someone, I recovered with no physical side effects and no obvious brain damage.

Although, some of my former school teachers might politely disagree on the latter. (Ha-ha!)

Laban's random lessons:

Parents! Install better gates for your children.

Well, that too, but the other obvious lesson here is as follows:

It's a bloody miracle that we are even here.

Life can be snuffed out without a moment's notice. If you were to die tomorrow, what would you hope you achieved during your time on Earth?

Would I have hoped to:

- Write that book?
- Climb that mountain?
- Forgive that person?
- Run that marathon?
- Lose that weight?
- Quit those ciggies?
- Date that person?
- Write that song?
- Leave a positive impact on the world?
- Made the world a better place?

*"Somebody should tell us, right at the start of our lives,
that we are dying. Then we might live life to the limit,
every minute of every day. Do it! I say. Whatever you want
to do, do it now! There are only so many tomorrows."*
—Pope Paul VI

MASSIVE ERECTIONS

You would think I'd be done with extreme needles by now, but I received another lumbar puncture seventeen years later whilst living and working in Bangkok, Thailand.

One rare Saturday off work, I was playing a nuggety half-back position for a local ten-a-side Rugby team.

At nearly 100% humidity and 43 degrees Celsius (approximately 109 degrees Fahrenheit, in case you're curious), the official temperature was rated "hotter than a camel's arse." My game came to a premature finish after I collapsed from heat exhaustion.

I awoke to find both my legs covered in hundreds of fire ants.

I now understand how they get their name!

Somehow, I played well enough to win *man of the match*. Although, in hindsight, maybe they felt bad for my unconsciousness.

I went out that night to celebrate with my victorious teammates and we all got blind drunk, mainly on locally made Carlsberg (that was preserved with a formaldehyde formula), and whole bottles of Jack Daniels mixed with cola and (hopefully!) purified ice.

After drinking myself into yet another expat-level stupor, I jumped in my chauffeured Toyota, driven by one Mr. Kong.

Mr. Kong, my driver, was a fifty-five-year-old Thai man who stood about 55 inches tall.

Many times, he would proclaim in his best yet broken English, that he had five wives, all of whom he complained about regularly.

He worked harder than the eighty-plus hours I was working, so I am buggered if I know how he kept that up!

Mr. Kong dropped me home and I fell into bed with all my clothes and shoes still on, neglecting to switch on the air conditioning.

Big mistake.

I awoke ten hours later with my tongue chemically stuck to the roof of my mouth. A quick inspection of the house revealed that I had zero drinkable water.

Tap water was out of the question, as no matter how thirsty I was, dysentery was never worth it.

As I trudged down to the local convenience store, I noticed a sharp pain at the base of my spine. Hangovers were bad enough, but when you add weapon-grade soreness to your coccyx, it becomes a brutal combination.

I had a tourist friend, Tim, arriving from overseas that night, so I swallowed some weird over the counter painkillers and grimaced my way through the day.

Tim was knackered from his flight, so we had an early dinner of locally made Khao Phat Gai (pronounced Cow Pat Guy—I've seen a guy pat cow, but never in reverse) and went to bed.

A vivid nightmare tore through my melatonin-soaked subconscious. I was in a fight for my life against a Knight of the Round Table.

In this match up, I swung my Excalibur, and it glanced off my arch nemesis's armour with a shower of sparks and dug itself into the dirt.

He countered with a shield-edge straight to my helmet. It knocked me onto my knees. The dark knight seized his moment and effortlessly pierced my exposed lower back with his broadsword, severing my spinal cord in two.

The paralysis woke me from my medieval hell and the first thing I noticed was the cool breeze from the air conditioning. But I was soaked in sweat from head to toe. Something wasn't right. Ouch! Why did my back still hurt so badly that I wanted to rip my spinal cord from the surrounding sinew and ligaments with my bare hands?

I hopped into the shower bath (shath?) and enjoyed some momentary relief as the warm water seemed to help.

I remembered I still had some weird pain medication and gulped down what remained.

By morning the pain was at DEFCON 1 and I needed serious medical intervention.

I arranged for Mr. Kong to pick me up and drive me straight to Bumrungrad Hospital (which means "to nurture the people" and not "diarrhea whilst jogging" like I originally assumed).

It's a beautiful, five-star hospital used by wealthy Thais and expats for all things medical, but especially boob-jobs and porcelain veneers.

I was rushed to see the orthopedic surgeon, as we all assumed it was a lower back injury from the weekend's game.

The orthopedic surgeon quickly referred me to the general surgeon after poking my tailbone with his stiff index finger. The ensuing pain nearly killed me and changed the diagnosis simultaneously.

A pilonidal abscess was found. Basically, a severely infected hair follicle right next to my anus.

The good news: they could operate on it immediately.

"Simply pay $5,000 USD, and we can do it right away, Mr. Ditchburn."

That was more than two months' wages for me, which I did not have. But not to worry! As part of my contract, my employer was entrusted to provide me adequate private healthcare and a suitable working visa.

Turns out, neither existed when I needed them most.

When my tourist visa was about to expire, I had to be driven to a shonky part of Patpong market and leave it for two days with some guy whose "immigration" office was located between a strip joint and a brothel.

When I picked up my passport, it showed arrival and departure stamps to a country to which I'd never been—Malaysia.

I called my boss and basically threatened him; the company needed to sort this out, or they would still have to pay $5,000 US to send my bloody casket back to New Zealand after I died. Talk about leverage.

The answer will always be no if you never ask the question and finally common sense was seen, and the money was paid.

A pus-filled and swollen two-by-two-inch hole was drained with expert medical precision and an extra small cordless vacuum cleaner.

Had they gone any deeper, they basically would have dug me a spare rectum. (*Rectum him? Damn near killed 'im!*)

I had pain relief this time in the form of an epidural.

Yes, the same injection given to women in labor—a practice western medicine avoids, when possible, as there is an associated high risk of accidental paralysis if it goes wrong.

I still remember the crunching noise it made when the long sharp needle was inserted into the fluid surrounding my spine. Gross.

Call me weird, but I have always rather enjoyed the whole experience of being operated on. I'm not sure why.

However, the whole experience was made a whole lot funnier after I politely requested to huff on the medical grade nitrous oxide in the operating room.

The nurse suggested I take small, shallow breaths. I took long, deep ones.

I laughed my heart out for the thirty minutes it took to complete the procedure; by the end, the rest of the surgical team had joined in via osmosis.

After comedy hour had worn off, I was wheeled off to the recovery room. My torso was still very numb from the drugs, and I was left on my back to let the numbing agent wear off.

Within fifteen minutes, two trainee female nurses approached my bedside to check up on my progress.

One nurse stood at the foot of my bed and inspected my chart whilst the other one grabbed at the warm blanket placed over me.

After peeling my bedsheet back, she revealed my nudeness to the world. Shocked, they both giggled embarrassingly before quickly replacing the sheet and disappearing off to another ward.

Curious to know what was so humorous, I lifted my sheet and revealed one very numb, yet proudly erect penis.

Unbeknownst to me at the time, one of the side effects of epidurals in men, is quite literally a massive erection. The more you know…

Laban's random lessons:

Don't fall asleep at the nude beach (no need to explain that one).

Laughter really is the best medicine.

Thailand really is a brilliant country to visit.

In life, sometimes you need to rely on your intuition and say yes to something you've never done before. Just because all this madness happened to me over there, doesn't mean for a minute that I would have changed my decision to accept the job offer.

Many of the "bad" situations I have ended up in, were due to the deliberate ignoring of my own gut instinct.

Try listening to yours next time and see what happens.

LAS VEGAS LAY

As a validation seeker, I would often use sex as part of my approval seeking process. Not surprisingly, when plied with alcohol, I sought out exciting sexual adventures like Pepé Le Pew might do if drunk on French wine.

One particular incident happened whilst on holiday in December of 2005.

Twenty-five years old at the time, we were visiting magical Las Vegas—famous for *Ocean's Eleven* and hedonism.

I'm a big fan of the movie franchise; but back then, I was an even bigger fan of the latter.

I was staying at the Bellagio Hotel with some colleagues, and we were celebrating a work incentive trip together.

After checking in, my acquaintances and I headed out for a typical over-the-top, lavish buffet dinner.

I often used food as a crutch and an all-you-can-eat buffet restaurant in Las Vegas was a great place to exercise those demons.

Having already committed three of the deadly sins at dinner (gluttony, greed, and sloth), I decided to maraud the rest of the hotel in an attempt to tick off the rest of that diabolical list (pride, envy, lust and wrath)

I found an intimate cocktail bar nearby and plonked myself opposite the barman.

"What will it be, sir?" he asked.

"Dry martini, shaken not stirred," I regurgitated back, using my very best Sean Connery impression.

He looked back at me with a large disingenuous smile, and I could hear his brain tabulate just how many times he had heard that line before.

By his exasperated response, it must've been in the thousands.

I differentiated myself by forcing an awkward joke on the now glazed-eyed barman.

"Sean Connery walks into a bar. He says, 'I'd like a s(h)ingle shot.'

"The bartender says, 'That's a good idea because if you had the chickenpox, the virus is already in you.'"

He didn't laugh and the joke didn't help. My only savior was the 35% tip I felt obliged to pay.

Over the next four hours, I consumed enough gin to maim a small elephant.

I was drunk, but lucid enough to know that I was far from done for the evening. I was ready to find that next crazy adventure.

Leaving the bar, I headed to the main casino floor to observe the landscape. The place was a hive of activity, lights, and excitement.

Even if you're not a gambler, it's a magnificent sight to behold.

Thousands of poker machines, alongside hundreds of tables, dotted with gamblers of all races and creeds—all vying for that Las Vegas luck.

Looking to my right, next to the blackjack table, I spied a fantastically presented trio: one man and two women.

They looked like they knew how to have fun, so I beelined straight towards them and introduced myself.

They seemed a little taken aback when I boldly approached them, but they soon realized I wasn't a threat and opened their arms, hearts, and minds to me.

Marty, Molly, and Vanessa were newly arrived from London in an escape of their own way, with the death of Marty's father only days earlier.

Marty was a flamboyantly gay and fantastic jewelry designer for British superstars like Kate Moss; Vanessa, a wealthy English socialite; and Molly, an artist and erotic novelist, former fashion editor of Harper's & Queen, and, after becoming a television personality, the first female banned by the BBC for swearing on TV.

It didn't take a rocket surgeon to realize I was in the presence of some pretty amazing people, who had lived some pretty amazing lives.

They asked me what I did, and I made up some malarkey

about being better than I was—and that I was a surfer.

The closest thing I've ever got to surfing was using Mr. Zog's Sex Wax to style my hair (before it fell out at age sixteen… probably due to the wax, now that I think about it).

They were all stone cold sober and had been for years. They didn't mind my drinking around them, and we enjoyed gambling across a few different tables, laughing and joking and generally enjoying each other's company.

I distracted them from the bad news back home; they distracted me from having to call it a night.

We spoke about many things that evening, but like most drunken discussions, the topic of sex came up, and each of us revealed how recent our last conquests had been.

As we went through our respective numbers, Molly, who was last, surprised everyone by admitting it had been a whole decade since she had been with a man.

(Although, she did reveal that some of her former lovers included Louis Armstrong, John Mortimer, George Melly, John Thaw, and Bo Diddley.)

"I'll break that dry spell for you, Molly," I interjected.

"Oh God, no," she responded sheepishly. "I couldn't possibly. Anyways, I'm much too old for you!"

"You're as old as the man you're touching," I joked.

She laughed and we headed to another section of the bar to take a better-positioned view of the casino.

I offered my services to Molly one more time and made

sure she knew I was serious.

Molly's eyes looked up and left, and her expression changed to one of pondering. She was thinking about it.

"Humph, I wish someone would ask me for a fuck!" Marty proclaimed.

We all laughed, and Vanessa snorted her drink out her nose. She was enjoying the to-ing and fro-ing but was staying well away from this discussion.

I sidled up next to Molly and got within striking distance for a kiss on the lips. I pounced like a panther, but she modestly deflected her face away at the last second and my lips landed on her cheek.

My second attempt was a success and I had landed a passionate kiss smack bang on her red cherry Dior painted lips, and the floodgates burst open.

She kissed me back, and I could tell this had a dramatic and positive effect on her.

I grabbed Molly by the hand, and we snuck off to the ambulant section of the men's toilet.

The romance happened and the deed was done without having to remove too much clothing and we soon returned to Marty and Vanessa.

Another notch on my belt, I thought to myself, before being startled back to reality when Molly asked if I'd like to join them for breakfast.

I was still very much intoxicated at that point, so I said,

"Of course."

I joined the trio for breakfast, and we discussed fondly what had happened.

Molly had broken her ten-year sex hiatus and I had helped her do it.

Win-win! I thought.

We exchanged contact details and before they left to retire for the day. I kindly suggested to Molly that if she ever wrote another erotic novel, she use "Laban" as a character name.

That would be cool, I thought to myself.

I had a late morning flight to New York to catch, so I trudged my way back to the room and packed my things.

After arriving in the Big Apple and sleeping off a powerful hangover, I awoke to the shame of doing something that, had I been sober, I wouldn't have done.

Molly was much older than me; to say I was ashamed was an understatement.

I didn't tell a single soul what had happened.

Another drunken event locked away in the "forgotten memory" banks of my brain.

Laban's random lesson:

Over my life, I have awoken the next day to many regrettable situations with women. Not that the ladies involved were bad people—far from it—it's just that the rule should at least be this:

- If you would not sleep with someone when you are sober, you should never sleep with them not sober. However, try telling that to a horny drunk who uses sex as escapism.

WELCOME TO MOLLYWOOD

Fast forward three years and I find myself back in Australia on a Thursday night, drinking beers with the lads.

And as the pints went down, so did the quality of the conversation.

Somebody in the group proposed a controversial question to everyone.

"How old is the oldest woman you've ever been with?"

We laughed awkwardly and then quickly scanned each other to see who would start us off.

Someone shared that he had pashed his boss's secretary who was fifty-six at the time, and we all laughed heartily and cheered our drinks in appreciation.

There were a few other half-hearted attempts, but nothing of any substance. So, I felt it was my time to contribute.

At this point, enough time had elapsed, and enough beer had weakened my tight lips for me to feel comfortable sharing my story.

"Gentleman, I think I can beat that," I said apprehensively.

"Go on then, Labes, what have you got for us?" they goaded.

I paused briefly, then executed.

"I made love to a seventy-three-year-old erotic novelist in a bathroom in Las Vegas!"

"What?!" they yelled disbelievingly.

"That's absolute bullshit, mate; you always tell us everything, and there's no way you could have kept that a secret this long!"

"I did, honestly lads, no bullshit… Her name was Molly Parkin."

"No mate, you're talking absolute codswallop."

"Just forget it then," I relented. They dismissed my pleas and the topic quickly changed to something slightly more mundane.

It was too unbelievable to them, but I was thankful for the brief reprieve.

I say brief because what happened next was truly shocking.

The next day arrived, right on schedule. Just like any other Friday morning, I was in the office doing my thing, when my phone started going bananas.

Ding-Ding-Ding! The text messages started flying through. Then came the phone call from my mate from the night before.

Before I could say anything, he yells, "Fuck me, Ditchburn; check your email, *now!*"

I hung up the phone and immediately jumped on my computer.

The subject line of the first email read: "What the actual

fuck!"

I clicked the link, and it opened a page on the *Daily Mail* (largely regarded as one of the biggest, and certainly the most scandalous, news sites in the UK).

Good golly, Ms. Molly!

"The flamboyant Molly Parkin, 75—one-time fashion editor, novelist and artist—reveals how an unlikely sexual encounter with a man 50 years her junior has inspired her to paint again."

And as I finished reading the sub-headline, the blood drained from my face, and I started to feel weak in the knees.

I scanned the article and my breath quickened.

There it was: "Laban."

In black and white, in a major newspaper. My name plastered all over the page.

Laban, it's an unusual name. In fact, I've never even met another Laban before.

You'll recall the moment at breakfast when I politely requested that my name be used should she ever write again?

Well, now I had my wish. Well, nearly.

My heart started beating faster than a John Bonham drum solo. My phone rang again, startling me.

"Jesus H. Christ, this is everywhere, bro. Check your inbox."

Ping! Another email came through.

This time with a link to *Wales Online*, the huge UK tabloid newspaper.

Again, I clicked on the link.

MOLLY REVEALS HOT AFFAIR IN LAS VEGAS, screamed the headline.

Author and artist Molly Parkin has revealed how a 'mystical' encounter with a young Australian man in a Las Vegas casino reinvigorated her lust for life.

I gasped out loud and then I could feel my brain politely ask me what to do; was it fight or flight?

Another email, this time from *Express.co.uk*, another major tabloid read all across the UK.

BOLD MOLLY BEDS TOY-BOY SURFER!, the headline declared.

You also recall the barefaced lie about being a surfer? Yeah, well, this is why we tell the truth, people!

The enormity of the situation caused my head to spin.

One simple Boolean search of "'Molly Parkin' and 'Laban'" triggered a huge bonanza of headlines from right across the globe. "Laban" was a mysterious gentleman.

Meanwhile, I was unanimously declared the winner of the *"who had been with the oldest woman"* competition and we could all go on with our lives.

Or so I thought.

My formerly sceptical friends now had the scoop on what

has been described by many as the "greatest story ever told" and it didn't take long for the gossip grapevine to swing into action.

Within days, people I had never met were asking me if what they had heard was true.

I must admit, I felt very uncomfortable admitting this to people, especially whilst sober. I mean, having a one-night stand was one thing, but having a one-night stand with someone fifty years older…

After all the madness calmed down, I took the time to actually read what had been written about Molly and me.

It turned out that when I met Molly in 2005, her life was at a low point considering her previously extravagant existence.

Basically bankrupt, and relying on others to survive, that tryst in a Las Vegas bathroom had reinvigorated Molly and sparked a new lust for life, creating a catalyst for change.

She resumed painting and writing—even tried her hand at being a DJ in clubs across London with her daughter and granddaughter. Not bad for seventy-odd years old.

Another few years passed by and after pressure from some friends, I decided to get in contact with Molly.

I dug through my old papers and found the ripped casino KENO card on which Molly had written her details. Even her handwriting was flamboyant and eccentric.

I timed the call to be a decent hour London time and rang the number.

"Hello, this is Moll," she answered.

"Hi, Molly, this is Laban. Remember me?"

The phone went silent for a few seconds and then she burst into voice.

"Laban! How lovely to hear from you!"

We spoke for nearly an hour and Molly was thrilled to share with me the wonderful progress she had made since we last saw each other.

Her career as a prolific painter had taken off again, and she was selling her artwork for tens of thousands of pounds in galleries across the UK and Europe.

She was most proud of her piece "Las Vegas Lay," a rendition of our encounter together. She even nailed my rather muscular thighs and proud buttocks.

It hangs to this day, in a private art gallery in Chelsea, London.

Not long after contact was made, I was approached by the BBC in England.

They were producing a documentary on Molly's colorful life, and they wanted to hear my side of the Las Vegas story.

I politely declined, as the gravity of my actions still shrouded me in shame.

Molly had also just finished her autobiography, *Welcome to Mollywood*[3], where she recounted her fascinating life from

---

[3] Molly Parkin, Welcome to Mollywood (London: Beautiful Books, September 26, 2014).

day one and decided to then dedicate a whole chapter to her Las Vegas experience with Laban, the blond surfer.

With Molly's permission and for your entertainment, I've included, verbatim, an extract from her autobiography. You may recall, Molly is an award-winning erotic novelist. So, I'll let you, dear reader, decide what is fact and what is fiction…

He skillfully slid one leg out of my underwear, after freeing it from my satin trousers, mercifully on an elastic waistband, which stretched for the onslaught, leaving the other half of my lumbar regions still fully clothed.

At 73, almost 74, I had never been so swiftly or so seductively semi-undressed, ever. Not ever. And this endeared me now to this total stranger, so that to facilitate easier entry, I planted my left foot atop the lavatory seat, cover down. Such that with every sensual lunge, an automatic response like the pulling of a chain to expel the contents of the lavabo occurred, as loud as a symphony concert.

We whooped in unison, roaring together, brimming with this added humor unexpectedly enhancing the occasion, bent double but still attached by our genitals. This boy was a sublime lover!

The orgasmic rapture was speeded up by the sounds of the cleaner approaching; clanging an enamel bucket and thrusting his mop under the door when it failed to open. We could barely contain our laughter, but contain it, we did.

Mesmerised by the action, to and fro, of the mop, we both climaxed together in silence. The atmosphere was electrifying. The cleaner retreated, banging the exit door behind him.

My lover kept coming. I had forgotten just how much spunk young men produce. Had I still been fertile, I would have conceived sextuplets or more, from that single insertion. It gives me a profound satisfaction to declare that this had been one of the more invigorating of my many sexual encounters.

One I still hold dear to my heart, which to this very day, writing this now, still brings a wide smile to my face. Proving indeed to be my sexual swansong.

Laban's random lessons:

Ha-ha, well you're probably wondering what obscure lesson is to come from this experience?. The honest reason I share this story with you is because it's too good not to share. It's also a great example of what happens when you speak the truth (well, eventually at least).

We all do and say things that are embarrassing and anyone who doesn't is either telling fibs or not really pushing the boundaries of living.

When we share these stories with people who love and respect us, it distributes the burden of knowledge and takes the sting out of storing in our complicated heads, where it ruminates amongst shame and anxiety.

Why do you think the Catholic confession booth is so popular?

SOBRIETY

I came to a realization in my latter years: whilst Mum and Dad grew up in totally different environments, they shared equally dysfunctional families.

Dad, one of four, grew up with parents who remained in a loveless marriage until all the children were full blown adults; and by then, the damage was done. The behaviors the parents exhibited to each other were horrendous and just hearing about it sounds like absolute hell.

My Mum, also one of four children, grew up with an alcoholic father whose verbal abuse when drunk was about as terrible as you can imagine.

With the benefit of hindsight, both sets of parents should have divorced the moment they realized they no longer loved each other, but that's not what people did in those days.

Staying together for the kids often does more harm than good in my observation, but equally there is some cold hard data that suggests a family split apart, does way more damage than a dysfunctional one staying together.

Nonetheless, I was determined to break this cycle no matter what and after several months of therapy with Lee, the shrink,

I was getting comfortable recognizing my emotions more, and some major healing seemed to have taken place.

My interest in gambling slowly dissipated and in December 2015, I just plain stopped.

And it felt so good to do so and I began to wonder what else I could give up.

In July of 2016, my younger brother, Josh, had been stone cold sober for nine months. A massive achievement for him. I remember moving from mockery to pride over a short period of time when I started to notice the dramatic improvements in the way he conducted himself.

His relationship with alcohol was not quite as dramatic as mine, but I had certainly witnessed enough firsthand experiences to know that he could probably do with knocking the frothies on the head.

Josh would usually just use alcohol as a relaxant, escape tool, and social lubricant.

He and his family lived in sunny Queensland, on the beautiful sunshine coast, and as a doting uncle, I would fly up and visit once every three months or so.

I initially noticed simple things like snapping at the kids (for just being kids) greatly reduced.

Any tension between him and wife eased, and our relationship improved dramatically.

The seemingly innocuous things that would cause huge arguments disappeared almost overnight.

Physically, his weight reduced, complexion improved, and the puffiness in his face subsided. Plus, raising a family on one wage, the extra money from not "*frothing*" was always welcome.

My twelve months of counseling, combined with Josh's voluntary sobriety, inspired me to take the plunge. So, that July I made the decision to stop cold turkey.

I didn't enter a recovery program or use anything other than willpower and it wasn't long before I received my first test from the universe.

A mate of mine invited me and a mutual pal up to Sydney to watch the famous All Blacks of New Zealand play Australia in a rugby grudge match that made it the must-see game of the year.

The offer was to attend the game in a corporate box owned by one of Australia's largest gambling companies, enjoy countless free beers, free betting coupons, and great company.

Talk about tempting fate.

I had successfully quit gambling seven months earlier and was five weeks sober when the game was due to play, and I graciously accepted under the following terms:

"I'll happily fly up and enjoy the game with you, but just letting you know I'm not drinking or gambling anymore, so if that's a deal breaker for you, I totally understand."

The answer was simply, "Of course, that's fine."

So, we booked our flights and away we went.

The day of the game arrived, and the city was buzzing with 80,000 fans from all over the world.

We met at a bar near the stadium, as we had a few hours to spare before we could hit the corporate box; of course, several orders were taken for drinks.

Everyone else ordered beer; I, a lemon, lime, and bitters (a sweet and sugary drink, but free from alcohol, nonetheless).

The first round was purchased by me, and I thought nothing of it when it was my host's turn to buy the next round.

I took a sip of the drink and noticed that it tasted a little different from the first one and immediately asked my mates what they had ordered me.

"Lemon, lime, and bitters, bro," they echoed each other.

"Nothing else?" I asked.

"Nope."

I shrugged my shoulders and quickly knocked back my drink, not realizing what had taken place.

I started to notice a familiar buzz from my many hundreds, if not thousands, of drinking encounters during my twenty-year drinking career.

I asked again about the contents of my drink and this time they couldn't contain their excitement.

"Two shots of voddie, bro!"

That's Australian slang for vodka, in case you're curious.

"C'mon, man, let's party! Free booze!"

I kicked on that night, made the most of the free bar, and

even got back on the drink the following day to deal with the brutal hangover.

The next day, I returned to Melbourne and started my second attempt at self-imposed sobriety on the twenty-sixth of August 2016.

But it took a few weeks for that whole affair to sink in; that single act of sabotage deeply affected me in a way that I didn't really expect.

I developed a real loathing and resentment for all parties involved.

I had my right to not drink taken away from me. Yes, I continued drinking that night and the next day—but that first drink wasn't my choice and for that reason I was well within my rights to be pissed off.

Since then, all parties involved have been forgiven, as there is no point expending energy on past wrongdoings.

What I have done going forward is try to include more people who provide real value in my life, give of themselves instead of taking, and lift me up rather than trying to tear me down.

Laban's random lessons:

I'm very proud to say that I haven't ingested a single drop, voluntarily or involuntarily since 2016, and have zero desire to do so.

Five years of no booze is normally a super-proud achievement for most recovering alcoholics. I don't know the exact percentages, but it's a very low number for people to make it that far.

But for me, since I was able to remove my desire to escape, it's been almost criminal how easy it has been to stop.

I certainly know that's not the case for many people, but the wonderful blessings in my life that have come about since quitting, I can't really count and the amount of dangerous, hurtful, and stupid shit I do now, is virtually non-existent in comparison.

If you have any hope of getting out of whatever rut you are in, especially in regard to addiction, start by getting rid of the people who won't support you when you ask. It might seem unfair or harsh, but you'll thank yourself in the future… trust me.

CURING THE INCURABLE

I was nineteen when I developed my first case of very painful indigestion.

If you've never experienced severe heartburn before, insert a blunt pen knife into your chest cavity and rotate it a few degrees.

I'm only assuming this is the pain you'll feel, as I've yet to be stabbed in the chest cavity.

If you're silly enough to try this, send your self-addressed legal letters to me directly and I'll come over and slap you myself!

To ease the pain, I consumed one antacid daily and the problem soon went away.

The next week the same symptoms came back, but the dose needed to be doubled.

Several more weeks went by, and I was mortified to realize I was consuming the equivalent of a high-school teacher's yearly chalk allowance via two packs of Quick-Eze a day.

Many times the recommended dosage, but a necessary evil as the pain developing in my chest was incredible.

I went to see the doctor and he immediately diagnosed me

as having gastrointestinal reflux disorder (or GERD).

GERD is a digestive disease in which stomach acid or bile irritates the food pipe lining. It's incredibly painful and left unattended is linked to esophageal cancers and other unpleasantries.

He assured me it was purely a genetic disorder and there was *nothing* I could do about it

"Simply a case of bad genes, unfortunately, Mr. Ditchburn"

I shrugged in agreement and the doctor prescribed me proton pump inhibitors (PPIs) which work to reduce the amount of stomach acid that is produced, supposedly lessening the damage on the esophagus.

I took the medicine as ordered and presto: All gone!

For the next seventeen years I took this "harmless" drug, safe in the knowledge that I was healed from my genetic affliction.

Plus, the medication boasted a clean record for thirty years and no long-term issues had come about, apart from the occasional benign polyp in the stomach.

With each new doctor, I asked about alternative options, advances in technology, or dietary changes that might allow me to come off the medication.

Each time I was told the same party line: "Genetic"… "Nothing can be done"… "Surgery is only fifty-fifty"… "keep taking the drugs."

Twenty different GPs, two surgeons, and two endoscopies

all revealed that same indoctrinated response.

One doctor suggested a colonoscopy to see what was going on in there.

"Well, whatever a colonoscopy is, Doc, you can stick that up your arse!"

I was getting frustrated at this point as I had started reading research papers that suggested these drugs were not as harmless as first thought.

After starting a laser-focused effort to heal my life—including the physical, emotional, spiritual, and mental components—I sensed that for my healing to really ramp up, I needed to start paying attention to my life in a holistic way.

A friend recommended I watch a podcast series called *The Joe Rogan Experience*, a weekly two-to-three-hour long interview format with literally thousands of fascinating guests over the last decade or so.

One episode especially caught my attention. It was an interview with Dr. Chris Kresser, a functional medicine doctor.

Dr. Chris spoke about the link between gluten intolerance and reflux disorders, and I found myself glued to the interview.

He explained that gluten is a group of proteins called prolamins and glutelins.

It's found mainly in wheat, rye, barley, and bulgur, plus a few others, and gives bread its stretchy consistency.

But there is another part involved, which contains another

protein called zonulin (which sounds like a Greek god, but it's not—though it causes an equal amount of destruction).

Zonulin is a protein that modulates the permeability of tight junctions between cells of the wall of the digestive tract.

To explain in layman's terms, it basically creates microscopic gaps in areas that are supposed to remain closed. The unprocessed food material enters the bloodstream having not gone through a proper digestion process and triggers an autoimmune response from the body.

In my case, it was heartburn. In many others, it's skin issues, joint pain, asthma, arthritis, eczema, psoriasis, irritable bowel syndrome (IBS), Crohn's disease, and they even think that some anxiety and depression illnesses are an autoimmune response at times.

I listened intently. *Hmm, I wonder if that's me?*

I went off to the local GP and took a battery of blood work and even got myself DEXA scanned to ascertain just how fat I really was.

A DEXA scan is an imaging test that measures bone density (the amount of bone mineral contained in a certain volume of bone) by passing x-rays with two different energy levels through the bone. It's used to diagnose osteoporosis (a decrease in bone mass and density) and it also reveals body fat.

And if you're someone like me, who always assumed you're "big boned," I have some shocking news for you:

You're actually fat.

Sorry, but it's time someone told you the truth. I wish someone had told me.

Your bones may be denser than most, but they are almost certainly the standard size for a human. The good thing about knowing this is that you can change it.

In three months of cutting gluten out of my diet, I lost three whole kilograms (6.6 pounds) of visceral fat that was stuffed in and around my organs.

My exercise routine hadn't changed, and I was eating around the same amounts of food, but I had excluded all wheat including bread, pasta, baked goods, and anything that contained this stretchy, salubrious sonofabitch.

My bloodwork also dramatically improved. The combination of weight loss and bloodwork was enough for me to know I was onto a winner.

Since that time, I kept off more than sixty pounds of weight, reversed my prediabetic state, added twenty-five pounds of muscle mass, and half a kilogram of skeletal bone density.

Quite remarkable by any doctor's standards and all of this was achieved without supplementation, steroids, or anything exogenous.

Even more interesting, in August of 2018, out of pure necessity, I had to remove all plants from my diet, and I adopted what is affectionately known as the "carnivore diet."

More of a lifestyle than anything else, it basically involves the best food-intolerance elimination protocol I've ever heard.

All you do is eat the best quality red meat, wild caught seafood, eggs, and dairy (if you can tolerate it) that you can afford.

That's it.

What? No plants; no fiber—how come you haven't died yet?

Well, do your own reading and this isn't medical advice, but at the time of writing, it's been over three years and I have had the most wonderful (less frequent) bowel movements, with virtually zero belching, bloating, or farting.

But don't just take my word from it. According to many peer-reviewed studies, it seems to work. Especially for people who have suffered from autoimmune issues stemming from "leaky gut," or intestinal permeability, as it is also known.

I have also experienced better mental health, virility, physical performance, and mood stability. Ask anyone who's known me for longer than five minutes and they'll attest to my energy, positivity, and general well-being.

I'm basically Benjamin Button, but with a ribeye.

Incidentally, I attribute the dietary shift to the dramatic improvements around my emotional healing and ability to avert relapse.

Fixing the gut, which generates 85-90% of the feel-good chemicals we use, seems to make a profound difference.

A very smart doctor at Harvard Medical School and Adjunct Professor that I interviewed on the *Become your own*

Superhero podcast, Dr. Chris Palmer, has been successfully putting one-third of all chronic depression, type 2 bipolar disorders, and schizophrenia patients into full remission, using the same ketogenic diet developed 120 years ago for epileptic children.

Another one third of patients significantly reduce their symptoms and medication.

The last third have no noticeable change, but if you're telling me we can improve at least 66% of the global mental health problems in the world by diet, this is something you have to take a look at.

This will ruffle a few vegans' fake feathers, but human beings, whether you believe or not, thrived for a very long time without plants. Just ask the Alaskan Inuit or Masai warriors of Kenya.

We are certainly omnivores by design; but damn, I feel good doing this.

I just keep getting better and better.

Coincidence? I doubt it.

Laban's random lesson:

If you asked me for just one piece of advice on what to do health-wise, it would be to remove the following items from your pantry and never buy them again: canola oil, corn oil, cottonseed oil, rapeseed oil, rice bran oil, safflower oil, soy oil, and sunflower oil.

Excessive amounts of omega 6 (linoleic acid) is starting to be linked to all kinds of chronic disease and the sooner you remove that gunk from your life, the better.

There is also some solid data and studies that suggest consuming as much organic food as possible (especially plants), can go a long way to mitigate glyphosate (a pesticide known as Round up) and deuterium consumption. I'm starting to go pretty deep now but a few of the recommended reading titles at the conclusion of this book go into much deeper detail.

Again, don't just take my word for it, check out some actual medical experts to help you make an informed decision.

HUGE EMOTIONAL BREAKTHROUGH

In early May 2018, I received a phone call from my older brother regarding yet another fight he had been in with my Mum.

What the actual argument was about I don't care to remember, but it involved both of them at each other's throats for what seemed like the millionth time and that sent me into a state of rage.

Not wanting to air others' dirty laundry in public, I'll leave it up to your very vivid imagination, but let's just say it involved something minutely trivial in the grand scheme of life.

I found myself (again) the person tasked with trying to resolve the situation, and I was furious at the prospect of having my peaceful evening disrupted.

Have you ever found yourself in the middle of a family dispute and felt the burden of responsibility?

Well, guess what I've figured out, it's not actually our job to fix anything!

By getting involved, we only exacerbate the issue, reinforce their behaviours and the cycle is allowed to repeat.

It took me over thirty-eight years to learn this, but when I did, let's just say it was damn sweet relief.

But back then, I hadn't figured that shit out yet and here I was AGAIN in the middle of a battle.

My brother was staying with my Mum at the time and the resulting argument finished with him being ejected onto the street—on his birthday no less.

I remember being so upset at the inconvenience of this all, I was physically shaking. So angry at the both of them that I wished for my own premature death, or theirs, whichever came first.

My usual train of behaviour would go something along the lines of this:

1. Send vicious text message pointing out how upset this was making me.
2. Follow up with verbally abusive phone calls and totally disrespect myself and my mother by bringing up past wrongdoings.
3. Send messages with totally regrettable comments that usually resulted in a six-plus month period of no-contact with my Mum.

Quick show of hands if this sounds like someone you know?

However, something was different this time around. Something was new and something was better.

During the course of the healing I was doing, I had absorbed more than two dozen books on anger, aggression, boundaries, stoicism, ownership, conflict resolution, triggers, shame, and family. And I was empowered with this new knowledge.

A sense of calm came over me like a warm wind you feel when exiting an aircraft and walking onto the tarmac of an exotic tropical destination.

My body switched into gear and started pulling all its resources from my brain like the Dewey Decimal classification system, only faster.

My brain concocted a brilliant (though never-before-tested) strategy.

Firstly, I would wait and allow myself the benefit of time and rationality.

Secondly, I would send my mother a message that she would never expect.

I wrote this the next day (which just happened to be Mother's Day):

Hey Mum,

Happy Mother's Day!

I appreciate what you did bringing me into this world and raising me the best way you knew how.

In August 2018 it will be two years since I had a drink and in December it will be three years since I last gambled.

I'm not perfect in what I do, but I've finally taken control of my life again and it's the most wonderful feeling I have ever experienced.

Physically, mentally, spiritually, I couldn't be happier. It's taken lots of hard work and effort, but I wouldn't have it any other way. I just want you to know that I wish you didn't grow up in that dysfunctional household like you did, but there is light at the end of the tunnel.

I know that you are in huge amounts of pain whether you know it or not and no matter the cause of all of this, it can be addressed, and you can live your life to the fullest extent.

I want a functional, happy, healthy relationship with my Mum and maybe it's my turn to take the lead on this. You've done so many wonderful things I can't even remember them all.

Who knows how long we have on this planet, so let's make use of this while we can.

I love you, Mum.
Labes.

I clicked send on the message and then noticed a physical weight lift off my body. It was so noticeable that I remember looking down at my left shoulder to see what it was that was causing such a feeling.

Nothing was there, but before my brain had time to register its confusion, my chest involuntarily heaved like a domesticated house cat right before it coughs up a giant, wet fur ball.

My body recoiled from the convulsion and my tear ducts switched open, drenching my face, and blurring my vision.

Salt water rushed onto my lips, and I burst into loud, guttural sobbing.

My sobbing was akin to sounds a mother might make after hearing news that her missing child has been found deceased.

That paints a ghoulish scene I realize, but despite how horrendous it sounded, it felt absolutely wonderful.

Completing a five-thousand-piece puzzle, hitting the winning runs for your team, getting an "all clear" from the doctor, or seeing a car-crash survivor walk away from an absolute disaster zone, still won't come close to how good I felt that morning.

It was close to thirty minutes of healing I'll likely never experience again, and I didn't know it was humanly possible to cry that much liquid.

I'm buggered if I know where that water came from after the first ten minutes, but if I ever figure it out, I'll have inadvertently solved any global water shortages.

Mum replied soon after and was genuinely surprised, yet grateful for the kind words. She told me it was the nicest message she had ever received from me.

Laban's random lessons:

Make peace with the people in your life that you need to forgive. Not for their sake as much as yours.

Pressure builds gradually—unnoticeable at first, but abundantly clear later.

Fun Fact: Science suggests that emotional tears contain additional proteins and hormones that aren't found in the two other types of tears. These may have relaxing or pain-relieving effects that help regulate the body and help it return to its normal state.

Maybe I should send more encouraging messages to people I care about?

How to Run a Marathon

The next seven days were unique to say the least. I was in very high spirits and felt like Bradley Cooper in *Limitless*, right after he ingests NZT, the drug that allows you to use 100% of your brain capacity.

A brilliant concept and a must-watch movie.

With the movie's theme song, "*Howlin' For You,*" playing in my headphones, I was strutting around the streets of Melbourne like a young John Travolta.

On that Wednesday, I headed into the city to see my favorite tailor, Mary.

I had dropped sixty pounds and gone from a 38-inch waist to a 30-inch waist over the previous months and amongst other things, needed my pants taken in.

Mary was a widowed Turkish, Christian woman, who had raised four children on her own after her husband passed away when she was just thirty-eight.

She had become an adopted grandmother to me and often I'd bring down coffee, and she'd listen to my crazy dating stories, or whatever insanity had been happening in my life that particular week.

"Hi, Mary!" I yelled down the escalator that delivered me into her studio.

"Laban, my boy," Mary smiled and threw her arms out to initiate a hug.

We embraced and shared several pleasantries before I noticed a beautiful young woman sitting next to an industrial sized sewing machine.

"Hi, are you Mary's friend?" I enquired.

"Oh… no," she gushed, "I'm waiting for the yoga studio to open up next door." Her huge smile revealed perfectly straight and shiny teeth.

"Oh," I said. "Are you into your health and well-being?"

"I am," she responded.

"Are you really?" Feigning disbelief, I asked again, producing my own cheeky smile.

She grinned from ear to ear and assuredly replied, "Yes, I am!"

My brain took over and said, *You just leave it with us, pal, we'll sort you out.*

I agreed and immediately my frontal cortex snapped into action, my mouth opened, and words flowed like Guinness on St. Patrick's Day.

"Well, I'd love to discuss health and well-being over a drink with you some time," I proposed.

After what felt like forever (though must have only been a few seconds), she replied.

"I'd love to !"

Boom! There it was folks, my first ever cold approach of a girl.

Stone. Cold. Sober.

"I'm Renae, nice to meet you," she said, extending her hand to me.

"I'm Laban."

Thirty-eight years of having to spell my name out to strangers kicked in. "L... A... B... A... N..."

"It means yogurt in Arabic... explains why I'm so cultured," I quipped, then awkwardly winked.

I didn't quite get the raucous laughter I was expecting, but it didn't matter by then.

"It's nice to meet you, Renae."

We exchanged numbers as the door to the yoga studio opened up.

Renae said her goodbyes and gracefully exited Mary's shop.

I looked around to see if Mary had been witness to what went on.

"Oh my God! You two are going to marry!" She declared prematurely.

Prior to having the courage to ask out a real-life human being, I had been prolific on the internet dating scene.

Using Bumble, Tinder, Happn, and Plenty of Fish, I had been on more than 150 first dates during the previous four years.

I was in two year-long committed relationships during that time, so it worked out to seventy-five first dates a year. Eat your heart out Drew Barrymore!

My professional career to that point had been in recruitment, so I used many of those learned skills to qualify my dating prospects.

As a result, I rarely had a bad date; however, the difference between meeting someone in real life versus online is very different, as you might imagine.

Online it's impossible to pick up on the vibration of the person, the scent of the person, eye contact, and pheromone responses that we have evolved to look out for.

I think that's one of the reasons why I never really connected with anyone in the online world.

But interactions with that many people had an upside.

You get really good at the art form of dating.

That's a handy skill for when you meet someone great (which we'll discuss later).

The date was booked for the following Monday. I had arranged to meet her for a drink in the city, with contingent plans for dinner, assuming it went well—this is a good tip for inexperienced daters, as it gives you an out if there is no spark.

I was over the moon with this outcome, and I spent the next ninety-six hours telling anyone and everyone that would listen about this amazing happening.

The weekend rolled around super quickly, and I found

myself wide awake at 4 AM on Sunday morning. I had slept beautifully and felt rested, but it was at least ninety minutes earlier than my usual waking slot.

I had awoken to messages from good friends of mine who were living in Scotland; rather than text back, I put the coffee on and rang their number.

The time difference suited beautifully, and we ended up chatting for over an hour. They had a new child to gush over, and I had just asked a girl out in public, so it was all go.

We finished up the call and I remember being so uplifted from such a great conversation that I just wanted to run.

Where or how far I had no idea, but who was I to argue?

So, I laced up my trusty dark blue Nikes with the white *swoosh* (they made me run faster).

I layered up with black woolen attire—a long-sleeve shirt, gloves, beanie, and man-tights.

Catching a glimpse of myself in the mirror, I realized I looked more like a woolen bank robber than a runner, but due to my recent weight loss I noticed the cold way more than usual. And after checking the outdoor thermometer, which registered *Colder than a Tibetan Tin Toilet Top*, I needed to prepare accordingly.

Fuelled by black coffee, bravado, and bustling enthusiasm, I surged out the front door and headed for the famous botanical gardens in South Yarra, affectionately known as the Tan.

It's set across thirty-eight stunning hectares (or, about

3,800 acres) that slope down to the Yarra River. It's full of native trees, garden beds, lakes, and lawns and it's bloody beautiful.

It also has a 3.827 km running loop which is complemented by one special section called "Heartbreak Hill."

Its name has a bark worse than its bite, but it's still a decent incline and has broken many a runner.

After a great start, I completed the first lap with relative ease and decided at *least* one more was on the cards.

I smashed that one, too, and looked down at my GPS to see exactly how far I'd traveled just to make sure.

There it was, in black and white: 7.6 kms. Wow, a personal best.

I asked myself permission to go again. My legs were numb from the chill, but still had plenty of power in them.

Go son! And I headed off for another lap.

Talking to yourself rarely looks great. But at 6 AM on a freezing autumn morning, the only other human in sight was a construction worker holding a Stop/Go lollipop sign.

We caught each other's eye and I instinctively yelled, "Good morning!"

She acknowledged me with a forced smile but said nothing. Mind you, holding a lollipop sign for non-existent traffic could hardly be much fun, and I suspect she was daydreaming of a new career choice right at that time.

After completing the third lap, I realized that I had run

nonstop for an hour. I still hadn't eaten anything and pondered how my body was generating all that energy.

Body heat and sweat was in abundance. I needed to remove some layers if I was going to continue.

I ripped off the drenched beanie and moist gloves, held them in my left hand, and started off on lap four.

Before long, lollipop lady appeared again and I spied an opportunity to solve my clothing problems.

"What's your name?" I yelled from thirty meters away.

Lollipop lady's gaze swung back in my direction.

"Debbie," she yelled back.

"Hi, Debbie, I'm Laban… are you going to be here for the next twenty minutes?" I cheekily yelled back.

"Yep, I'll be here all bloody day at this rate," she scoffed.

"Would you mind keeping an eye on this for me?" I presented her my drenched items like a small wet sacrifice.

"I'll guard them with my life," she joked, as she fashioned her lollipop into a giant sword and made impressive striking motions like she was auditioning for Tarantino's *Kill Bill*.

"Thank you so much, you're a bloody legend!" I yelled as I lobbed the soaked goodies towards her before bounding off like Old Yeller.

Debbie was chuffed. She had new purpose in her position that day and I found someone to coat-check my goods, so it was a win-win as far as I was concerned.

The effect of Debbie's kindness triggered an unusual feeling in the pit of my stomach.

As I bounded off, I felt a surge of emotion come over me. Before I knew it, I was weeping profusely. Tears flowed again like the previous Sunday when I had texted my mum, but this time around they were tears of joy and not anything more sinister.

I continued to run as my face shed wave after wave of emotion and it lasted well over five minutes.

What the hell was happening to me?

Is this what a breakdown feels like?

Was this normal in distance running; had I missed all the memos talking about when you cry like a goddamn baby?

I immediately dismissed a breakdown scenario, as this felt way too good for something usually associated with a bunch of negative stuff.

Then it struck me.

A book I had recently read (*The Body Keeps the Score* by Bessel van der Kolk[4]) spoke about how trauma's resulting stress harms us through physiological changes to body and brain, and that those harms can persist throughout life.

The challenge of recovery is to re-establish ownership of your body and your mind—of yourself.

This means feeling free to know what you know and to

---

[4] Bessel van der Kolk, *The Body Keeps the Score* (New York: Penguin Books, 2015).

feel what you feel without becoming overwhelmed, enraged, ashamed, or collapsed.

For most people this involves finding a way to become calm and focused; learning to maintain that calm in response to images, thoughts, sounds, or physical sensations that remind you of the past; finding a way to be fully alive in the present and engaged with the people around you; not having to keep secrets from yourself, including secrets about the ways that you have managed to survive.

Maybe all of this self-development work was paying off? I was feeling alive in a way that I never had before.

Maybe my body was healing in ways I never really considered?

Maybe my body was physically purging stored emotion by way of running?

The tears switched off almost as fast as they started, and a surge of energy coursed through my veins.

I tore through the next 2 km in my own record pace, and before I knew it, I was done with lap four.

At a nearby fountain, I lapped back my first mouthfuls of water like a thirsty Labrador. The fountain was set on "fire engine" pressure level and the water sprayed all over my shirt and face like I'd just been hit square on the face by a water balloon.

The mix of fountain, sweat, tears, and God knows what else had taken its liquid toll on my long sleeve woolen top.

I peeled off my shirt with David Hasselhoff- like ease and wrung out what I could. Shirt-juice spilled forth and splashed down onto my blue shoes like a baby baptism. I revealed my newly crafted physique to the world for the first time totally sober.

During my drinking days, it wasn't uncommon to show off my beer belly, but I'd never done it sober, outside of the beach. And heaven forbid I'd ever be one of those wankers that ran with their shirt off!

But there I was, topless; and honestly, I didn't give a rat's arse.

From a fatigue perspective, surely, I was done.

Surely, I needed to stop, eat, and drink before my body exploded with overuse.

Nope.

I took off again and attacked Anderson Street hill like a reluctant kamikaze pilot, keen to look at it, but not actually wanting to go ahead with it.

I summited the street and headed back around towards Debbie's lollipop.

As I got within striking distance of my clothing stash, I yelled out to Debbie for some rhetorical advice.

"One more lap?" I asked, throwing my wet clothing onto the other pile.

Debbie was invested in this now, and in the process, had become my biggest and only fan.

"Hell, yes!" she said.

I finished six total laps of the Tan that day—five more than ever before, and when you include the distance to and from home, I had notched up a rather impressive 24 km of running. That's 19 km longer than my previous best and the only reason I stopped was because I was starving.

Runners talk about *hitting the wall* or *bonking* which is when you deplete all the stored glycogen in your muscles and liver. I guess I must've been awfully close to that, but after smashing down some steak and eggs, I found the energy to complete 100 sit-ups, 100 squats, and 100 pull -ups via a few separate sets of twenty.

My energy levels were off the Richter scale and I was just fizzing with oomph.

"I'm going to run a bloody marathon!" I squawked to my invisible audience; my voice hoarse from running.

My whole life, I have been incredibly impulsive and that day was no different.

I ripped open my laptop and furiously typed "next available marathon."

"Traralgon Marathon" flashed up as the first and only option.

AUSTRALIA'S OLDEST 42.2 KM RACE AND ONLY TWO AND A HALF HOURS FROM MELBOURNE! The headline proudly declared.

I booked and paid for that race faster than it took me to

find the thing online, but when the confirmation email came through, my heart sank.

Congratulations for joining us on June 3rd, 2018.

"Jesus H. Christ!" I yelled horrified.

It was fourteen days away and I didn't know the first thing about running that far!

My next internet search was medically focused.

Can you die from running too far too soon?

What happens to your body when you run a marathon?

Will I still be able to have children after running a marathon?

My mind raced and my heart pumped, and I wondered how the hell I was going to pull this one off.

P.S. You're probably wondering what happened to that girl from Mary's shop?

She cancelled the date on me. About 8 PM on Sunday evening, long after my big run and marathon confirmation email had been sent.

She told me she had recently gone through a major breakup and was still not over her ex-partner.

I was naturally disappointed, but wished her well and moved on with my life.

I actually found out the real truth more than three years later.

My lovely tailor friend, Mary, snagged the scoop straight from the horse's mouth.

Mary had been badgering the poor girl and reminding her frequently that she had missed a great opportunity in dating me. She finally cracked and said that in preparation for her date with me, she'd jumped online and did some research. There's quite literally only one Laban Ditchburn on the planet, so it wouldn't have been hard.

She saw something I posted on social media of which her mother wouldn't have approved.

I'm guessing if she ever reads this book, whatever off-color joke I posted back then, will seem pretty tame compared to the rest of the carnage written in here. Ha-ha!

The date going ahead never actually mattered. What Renae didn't realize was that she had sparked something wonderful in me. For that, I will be eternally grateful.

Posterity dictates I share this rare journal entry dated right around those specific events.

Written mainly in case I ever felt down on myself.

Today I live for the first time.

Today I wept whilst running.

Today I entered my first (of many) marathons, scheduled two weeks from today.

My mind is sharp, focused, and powerful.

My language is deliberate and measured.

Last Wednesday I asked out a stunningly beautiful woman who said yes! And then she cancelled a few days later. Something like this would ordinarily ruin me, but now I am the author of my own life's novel, and I decide what hurts me and what doesn't.

I'm currently Bradley Cooper in Limitless, my mind is a weapon that is only used for constructive powers. I will continue to practice mindfulness and being in the present.

I will continue to be authentic to the best of my abilities and not be afraid to polarize those that are not aligned with my core values.

My family is my light and new number one priority. Not to try and fix, but to be a pillar of strength and an example people can be proud to associate with.

Laban, for the first time you can remember, you are able to genuinely love who you have become.

My new goals are as follows:

I want to be a guest on the Joe Rogan podcast as an expert on kicking ass in life.

I want to become known as the world's happiest human being (sorry Matthieu Ricard)!

I will use my experience to inspire and encourage all those that come into my atmosphere.

I will remain grounded, humble, and gracious from this moment forward.

I will continue to offer love, connection, comfort, and an ear to listen to those who are open to self-improvement.

I will nourish my body with what God intended and reject the negative influence of food I know is not conducive to my continued joy and well-being.

Your finances will explode with success and abundance if you stay true to yourself.

Believe in your destiny, your life will continue to be blessed.

Continue to push new boundaries each day and lead like King Arthur.

Continue to document all the success in your life and embrace the lessons as they are your building blocks to life.

Laban, if you are reading this in a moment of weakness in the future when a major trauma has happened, remember this moment when you were lying face down on an angle, in your bed, using your phone as a touch resting on the pillow, having just entered your first Marathon and winning at life.

Remember this euphoric feeling that you have and the unstoppable mindset.

Continue to surround yourself with the best people possible.

Laban, you have grown into a man that any person would be proud of.

Laban's random lessons:

Write in a journal.

Documenting important parts of the journey allows me to be transported back to that very moment when I'm down or losing my way.

It's shown me now how much I've grown. I certainly forget at times; but those words remind me of what I'm grateful for and the amazing moments I have had in my life.

I can't express the importance of writing down these moments in our lives and even if you're not a daily writer, even the odd entry here and there will provide some much needed context when you need it most.

"When your mind tells you it's quitting time, you are actually only 40% spent." David Goggins, famed madman, ultra-runner, badass, Navy SEAL, Ranger, and possible cyborg

FORTY-TWO POINT TWO

Let's jump ahead.

Fourteen days later, on a perfectly still, zero Celsius day in Traralgon, Australia, I lined up with seventy-six other competitors to take on what would be the race of my life.

Not wanting to tackle it alone, I asked at least one hundred separate people in the lead up if they'd like to join me.

Unsurprisingly, I didn't get many takers. Not many people have a marathon worth of training ready to go like that, and the ones that did, probably didn't fancy running with such a novice liability like I presented.

At least half a dozen of them told me I was going to die on my feet, as training for this took many months and was reserved for seasoned runners.

However, at the eleventh hour, I was able to convince one young man to embark on this journey of discovery with me.

Enter the great hope, Dr. Sam Skinner.

Dr. Sam had what I call huge "dino-balls" (because what's bigger than regular balls?) and was a great mate of mine from Melbourne University Cricket Club where we had played together for over a decade.

Sam was only seventeen when he arrived at the club and he hailed from "God's country" in regional Victoria.

A Mildura boy, he was raised right. If you ask anyone who knows him, he is the epitome of what you seek in a mate: honest, reliable, (annoyingly) humble, with strong values and boundaries; someone who always tries to lead by example.

Unlike me, who until my transformation had pretty much displayed the opposite!

However, we had become unlikely pals, and this was a great get for me.

Sam had enjoyed a quiet eight months doing bugger all physical activity whilst trying to finish his PhD, but he had readied himself for this ginormous effort by running 27 kms the Thursday prior.

Unknown to me at the time, he was still incredibly sore from his jaunt, and we were both easily identified by the other runners as being "massively undercooked."

As referenced earlier, the Traralgon Marathon is the oldest race in Australia, but it's also the most boring. It's 42.2 km of flatness that never really lets up.

Don't get me wrong, it's fantastically organized and the people are magnificent, but that doesn't stop it from being the least inspiring location of any long-distance event. Plus, the gravel is just big enough to inflict pain on the thickest soles-and the local herds of cattle make for a terrible cheer squad.

Sam and I had a gentleman's agreement that was a "no man left behind" scenario.

It was a kind of insurance for us both, I suppose.

Sam had run this distance before, but it was more than eight years ago; a lot happens to the body during that time.

The starter's gun went off and so did we, allowing the elite runners to lead the way and forge a trail for us novices.

Sam's wife (who had completed her own personal best of 10 km with zero training) ran our support crew, yelling from the sidelines.

But the initial fanfare wore off pretty quickly and the next thing you know we were in the middle of farmland with just our thoughts and each other.

We set a decent pace early on, as our goal was to try and complete the run in under four hours. To give you some context, less than 25% of all marathon runners finish under that magic time, with many more not finishing at all.

We made it past the halfway mark unscathed, but soon after Sam started showing fatigue. Being the incredibly humble man he was, he finally admitted that he had been sore from the start. He had kept a brave face to this point, but the cracks were showing.

A mutual cricket mate, Hugh Van Cuylenburg, was the founder of a wonderful initiative called the Resilience Project. He and his equally wonderful wife, Penny, had generously arranged for several emblazoned singlets for Sam and I to wear on the run. The least we could do was use those damn principles!

Specifically, gratitude, empathy, and mindfulness (GEM); tools that when used well, are incredibly effective at improving one's mindset and well-being. Something both Sam and I needed at that moment.

They say a good marathon pace is one you can hold a conversation to. So, I did just that. I still had loads of energy and did most of the talking whilst Sam trudged along, putting one foot in front of another.

I went on about how blessed we both were to be out here doing this, whilst less fortunate people didn't get these types of opportunities. We both spoke about how lucky we were to have such great mates who would do something so inspiring for each other and it really made a massive difference to the overall mood.

My now patented crying-whilst-running had returned and that seemed to distract Sam from his failing legs. Having a grown man cry next to you for kilometers at a time seems to have that effect.

Now, don't think for a second that I was getting off the pain scot-free.

I was entering uncharted waters myself and once we hit the 30 km mark, my shit started to go south.

Marathon trivia fact #27: On average, your feet will contact the ground 43,000 times during a marathon.

First, anything hurts when you do it 43,000 times in a row (although, strangely, it didn't seem to affect Mum's arm with the wooden spoon).

Second, if not well conditioned, your calves will reward you with searing pain as the muscle fibres slowly tear apart.

Calf pain combined with feet pain works in a similar way to compound interest accumulating in Warren Buffett's bank account. It's fucking everywhere and it doesn't stop... ever!

Third, your quads will catch fire and then send emergency signals directly to your brain telling you to, firstly, go f*&K yourself, and then please stop, please.

All of those Sam and I chose to ignore, so right on cue, the fourth pain kicked in.

The fourth pain is not where you'd expect it, but it still hurts like fark.

You've probably never noticed the elbow flexor before—it's a muscle inside your forearm. That poor bugger cops an absolute hiding, as when you're swinging your arms 43,000 times, it tends to wear out.

It feels as though you've been lugging six supermarket bags jam packed with sand all afternoon. And it's not like you can stop using your arms when you run (unless you're C-3PO).

People who don't run a lot tend to say the same types of statements.

"Why would you do it to yourself?"

"I could never run that far."

"You're insane."

"I'll run to the pub."

"Why?"

I know this because I used to say those things, too.

But something strange happens when you run, and it can't be adequately described using English, in my opinion.

Many centuries ago, in the plains of Africa, human beings would run the equivalent of two marathons in one day to hunt and kill animals to eat.

Most animals can't sweat like us humans, and so we would chase those animals and tire them out until they literally collapsed.

Running 80+ kms for dinner seems pretty extreme, but that's what we used to do and do it well from all accounts.

Sam and I already had our dinner sorted that evening, so all we were burdened to do was to complete the damn run.

We clicked over the 35 km mark on pure adrenaline and mindset. We had come too far to pull out this late in the game and we kept reminding each other that "pain is temporary; pride is permanent."

If you've completed a long distance run, you'll easily empathize with this story so far, but if you haven't, then hopefully you'll be inspired to, because the next part gets good.

Sam was in total agony from what I could tell. His movements were labored, and his bright disposition had morphed into the face of someone who had just been told he had twenty-four hours to live.

I was in pain too, but nothing compared to Sam's situation, and it was up to me to help drag us over the line.

Our race pace had been great at the start and had built us a fantastic platform for the back half of the race. I double checked the estimated finish time and it read four hours and one minute based on our current plodding.

I yelled at Sam, "Bro, we've got a crack at a sub four-hour time, but we need to go just a little faster!"

He died a little more inside but cracked a smile, and managed to nod in agreement.

As I cried more tears of joy, we lifted our cadence by just a few more steps per minute.

As we passed through the final drinks station of the run, I plunged my fist into the lolly bowl and extracted half a kilo of sugary jelly snakes. I swung my mouth open and poured in enough to choke a small bear.

The sugar hit seemed to help for about thirty seconds, before my blood sugar crashed, and huge waves of lethargy washed over me like weighted wind.

The amount of shit that flows forth from our brains when we put it through that kind of misery is astonishing. I had so many voices that I didn't even recognize. They told me to stop and quit more times than I care to remember, and I'm sure Sam heard the same.

Our burst of enthusiasm earlier had helped knock several

minutes off the proposed finish time and optimism levels were at an all-time high.

We clicked over the 41 km mark and could see the finish in the distance.

One bloke in front of us missed the turn off through pure exhaustion and added another thirty seconds to his run before generous onlookers yelled through his noise-cancelling-head-phones and alerted him to the issue.

Sam and I were delirious with pain, joy, agony, pride, happiness, relief, and a multitude of other emotions as we passed over the finish line together, arm in arm as we had committed to each other.

Three hours, fifty-six minutes, and forty-seven seconds.

We had done it.

Sam collapsed into Jo's arms and I, into the pavement. My calf muscles twitched involuntarily. From where I sat, it seemed like thousands of tiny insects were crawling beneath my skin.

The race director placed our finisher medals around our necks and shook our hands proudly. "Well done, lads," he said. "Phenomenal effort."

The three of us drove back to Melbourne later that day swelling with pride. I, being the dating machine I was back then, had arranged dinner with a beautiful lady for later that evening.

I had no idea of how I would feel post run, so she was

surprised to hear from me, and happy that the date was still on.

We met for a drink and then headed across the road to a favorite Melbourne steak joint.

I destroyed over two kilos of ribs, steak, and pork belly during our date; had we gone Dutch on the bill, I'm sure she would have felt justifiably ripped off. I think she was more impressed that I could walk, let alone date and we finished the night with a pash. Not a bad effort considering the day's events.

Steps for the day: 53,000.

Money spent on date: $153.

Laban's random lesson:

I'm just going to quote Marcus Aurelius here, because he's more on point than me.

> *"Because a thing seems difficult for you, do not think it impossible for anyone to accomplish."*

HOW TO AVOID JAIL RAPE

A day after the race, my legs were still sorer than Hillary Clinton after the 2016 election, but this new powerful drug had taken a hold of me. And fast.

To quote Renton from the cult Scottish drug film *Trainspotting*, "I need one more fucking hit!"

June 3, 2018 was the day I completed my first ever marathon and June 4, 2018 was the day I signed up for my first ever ultramarathon.

The Surf Coast Century 100 km trail run, set in the stunning surf coast of Victoria, Australia, was my new outlandish goal.

The Surf Coast Century is one of ten essential Australian and New Zealand ultramarathon races and is widely referred to as a "must-do" race on the Australian running calendar.

Of the run, 22 kms is on the beach and the rest of the event combines 2,000 metres of elevation and challenging single trails that demand respect. It's one of only a few races in Australia that allows an opportunity to qualify for a prestigious ballot entry into the Western States 100, one of the most brutal races in North America.

A quick search online suggested a minimum of twelve to eighteen months to prepare to complete a distance that long. That was assuming you had a decent platform with which to start.

That's what I love about guides. That's exactly what they are—a guide. Like eating chicken one week after the expiry or popping some long-expired Viagra, it might end badly or you may just have a great night!

Three weeks earlier, 5 kms had been my best distance, so adding another 95 kms on top was going to take some planning.

I found another race to get some of the required practice in. A 50 km ultra run that involved thirteen laps of the famous Tan mentioned earlier, simply called "Tan Ultra."

It was set for three weeks out, on the twenty-fourth of June, three days before my thirty-eighth birthday. Given my recent success, I was very confident I could knock this off, but it was still a decent increase in distance given the short time frame.

The day arrived faster than expected, and again, I found myself at the starting line of a brand-new challenge.

The vibe at the race was great and I was in a particularly good mood as I had started a whirlwind romance a week earlier with a girl I had met on the local bus. Let's call her Casey.

We had been on five dates in seven days, and it was getting hot and heavy quite quickly.

She must have really liked me, as she offered to come and

watch me run after she finished moving to her new house.

Watching amateur runners for hours on end doesn't usually fall into the riveting entertainment category, but I certainly appreciated the sentiment and was grateful for the support. Plus, if I died on the track, at least she could collect my things for me.

Casey was moving four hours from Melbourne for a tree change employment opportunity; rather than focus on a future together with a long-distance commute, we were simply enjoying being in the moment.

She estimated her arrival over a few hours, so I knew she was going to come down at some point, but I wasn't sure when.

The race involved multiple laps of the same track; I'd easily be found, so I just got on with the race.

The starter snapped wooden blocks together like an enthusiastic parent applauding their child at a local swim meet.

I'm assuming the use of a proper starter's pistol in such a built-up posh neighbourhood, would have resulted in the deployment of an armed SWAT team, abseiling down the giant trees surrounding the park, and shooting out the knee-caps of the runners.

This time around, I had planned my run with much more thought. Ample food, drink, and clothing were coordinated weeks prior to the race, so all I needed to worry about was getting over the line.

The day started slightly overcast but the temperature was

good for a run, and I was grateful it wasn't raining.

I used audiobooks, music, and a few phone calls to help pass the time and before I realized it, I had knocked off 35 km.

My body had become well-adjusted to these distances and my legs felt really good until I hit the 40 km mark. The pain wasn't anywhere near as bad as Traralgon, but it still knocked me around a bit.

I pulled into my homemade pit stop and fuelled up on coconut water and a few premium Medjool dates. With all my health focus of late, I was determined to avoid processed sugar, which is usually all that's available at these types of events.

The volunteers holding the bags of candy were stationed every 1 km or so and their enthusiasm was infectious.

One lady vigorously offered me the treats ten times in a row, one for each lap, and each time I politely said, "No, thank you."

I made one more loop of the track and headed down the main straight where, just like clockwork, the treat lady was holding her bag and preparing her inevitable sales pitch to flog her free candy.

Running on pure instinct, I was politely telling myself to plough on.

As I approached the candy lady for the eleventh time, Casey appeared from behind her.

"Casey!" I yelled. She looked up at me and smiled.

Instinctively I immediately went towards her with a big,-

goofy, sweaty smile on my face.

Before she could say anything, I planted a massive smooch straight on her lips and embraced her like a long-lost love.

But something didn't feel quite right about this embrace, or her lips, so I pulled back to investigate.

The person standing in front of me suddenly looked nothing like Casey and the horrified look on her face confirmed she was not Casey at all!

I had just sexually assaulted some poor innocent bystander who was probably watching the race of a relative or heaven forbid her partner. Either way she was watching under duress anyways.

This was probably the last thing this poor woman needed!

"Oh my God, I'm… I'm so sorry!" I blurted out. "I thought you were my girlfriend."

Because trying to explain that I had only met Casey one week earlier and she was not my girlfriend yet, was WAY too complicated to explain at that point.

The poor woman was still in shock and still hadn't said anything. Maybe she was trying to remember where her can of mace was or was fossicking in her pockets for that illegal taser gun she picked up at Patpong market in Thailand the previous summer.

The lady dishing out the candy witnessed this assault first-hand, but she soon twigged on to what had happened and burst out laughing. I'm glad someone thought it was funny.

Runners often experience hallucinations or periods of disorientation when running very long distances, especially those as inexperienced as I was.

But I was faced with an awful dilemma. I was still competing in a race, albeit against myself, but I had paid good money to enter this comp and I was obliged to finish it.

I continued to apologize as I ran backwards in the direction I needed to go; within 200 meters I was around the corner and out of sight.

Then panic set in. When your nervous system is already on high alert due to the physical challenge you are putting it through, the last thing you need is the thought of being bundled up into a divisional police wagon at the start/finish line of an ultramarathon.

If I was declined bail and incarcerated overnight, I surely wouldn't have the physical strength post-race to fight off a prison rapist. Within minutes I would be somebody's prison bitch!

My brain was overloaded with stress and I called the only person I knew who could talk me through this.

Sam Skinner. Yes, the marathon man.

He took the call and was in high spirits as they had just put an offer in on their first home.

But Sam sensed the urgency in my voice and asked what was wrong.

"I've just sexually assaulted a complete stranger whilst

running a race!" I said. "I thought it was the girl I'm seeing, but it wasn't even close… how do I know what is real and what's not anymore?"

Sam was calm and quick to quell my fears. "Don't worry about it mate, just apologize when you see her next. I'm sure she'll understand."

He was so calm under fire. Here I was dreading my worst fear—prison rape—and he was as cool as a cucumber.

I ran with apprehension as I entered the main straight of the race where the alleged assault had happened.

Within a few minutes I could see ahead the parties involved and thankfully there was no major police presence yet.

Maybe they were still on their way, I catastrophized.

The woman I assaulted was almost within earshot. I took a deep breath and prepared to launch my apology again from a safe distance.

We locked eyes and I saw her break into a huge smile.

"That kiss was an eight out of ten!" she yelled out.

"And I expect the next one to be a ten out of ten!"

You can't possibly imagine the relief of hearing such beautiful words. My spirit lifted and I joyously yelled back.

"Thank you for not pressing charges!"

This acquittal ignited a flame inside my body and the fogginess and fatigue experienced earlier dissipated immediately.

I finished that damned 50 km in five hours and seven minutes flat, plus I retained my prison virginity in the process.

Phew.

Casey arrived thirty minutes after I finished the run and was later in hysterics as I relived the story. Being the dating machine I was, I helped Casey finish moving the last of her things and then we headed back to my apartment for dinner.

I'm pretty sure I got a kiss that night also! Two in one day.

Laban's random lessons:

- Making genuine mistakes won't always end in jail time.
- Staying positive in stressful situations always trumps the opposite.
- Seeking counsel of people that you can trust and rely on is paramount.
- Ultra-distance running might be a great substitute for psychedelics.
- A good dose of grace for others and a sense of humor does wonders

Born Again Virgin

Casey's and my whirlwind romance ended almost as fast as it started and before long, I was back to bachelorhood.

I had long since deleted all of my dating apps, so my usually constant flow of companionship dwindled to virtually nothing.

But this was an opportunity for me to focus on myself. Plus, I had less than six weeks to prepare for the race of my life (again).

I threw out multiple Hail Marys to people I thought might come on the run with me, but if bugger all people will run a 42 km with you, you could imagine the stone-cold silence of a 100 km!

I had proposed the question to Sammy Skinner back in July, but he was getting married in early 2019 and Jo, his fiancée, expressed major concern for his life after reading one of many stories on the internet about people dropping dead on long-distance runs.

Sure, it happens, but it's bloody rare and the main reason for dying is due to a condition called *hyponatremia*. That's when you drink so much water that you actually die of dehydration due to lost electrolytes. Helluva way to die mind you, but very unlikely… At least, that's what I told the both of them.

He said he'd keep working on convincing Jo as much as himself.

Fair enough, I suppose. Even with all my bravado, I couldn't guarantee I'd survive, let alone anyone else.

Sam kept me hanging on tenterhooks for over a month until that fateful day in August when he sent me a screenshot of his confirmation of booking for the 100 km run!

"Thank you, God," I breathed loudly.

Sam and Jo weren't the only people in their family that had a massive impact on my life.

During a conversation with Sam in late 2017, I randomly asked him if he knew of a decent life coach he could recommend.

It turned out Jo's mum, Dolly, was one and, although she was based in Mauritius, she could provide tele-coaching as good, if not better, than an in-person chat.

My six months with Dolly was life changing. She taught the importance of goal setting and reframing negative situations to positive. She also kept me accountable during a period in my life that was incredibly tumultuous.

That tumultuous period happened after I fell in love with a woman named Tulip (at least, that's what we'll call her).

Tulip and I met speed dating in September 2016, two

weeks after I had quit alcohol.

She was unlike any woman I had ever met at that point—kind, calm, and non-judgemental.

Speed dating whilst sober is something else, I assure you, but thankfully Tulip wasn't a big drinker. Before long, our love blossomed, and I was smitten with my "African Queen."

After five weeks of courting, Tulip called me up and told me that she had something really important to tell me, but it had to be in person.

My mind raced with all sorts of terrible scenarios including her revealing that she had acquired a whole suite of incurable STDs or that she was a man underneath all those clothes. We hadn't done anything more than kiss at that point, so everything was on the table.

"I'm a virgin," she quietly whispered to me. "And I'm saving myself for marriage."

"OK," I breathed a huge sigh of relief.

"I totally understand if you don't want to wait for me, and please take a week to think it over before making your decision."

I made my decision instantly.

I was in.

All of my previously failed relationships had involved jumping into the cot way too early and look how that had turned out.

"Tulip," I gushed. "I waive my weeklong decision-making

process; I love you and I'll do whatever it takes to make you happy."

Revisiting that moment triggers a gag reflex in my throat.

Not because of Tulip's right to save her virginity till she was ready, but for my total lack of consideration for my own very important needs.

I was a red-blooded male who had just removed almost all of the negative habits in my life that might curb a libido; so, as you might imagine, I was now hornier than ever.

Our honeymoon period lasted about three months, before my dark side reared its ugly head.

We got into a fight over her rejecting me for sex after an evening of heavy petting.

But Laban, she told you she wanted to save herself for marriage? I hear you cry!

Yeah, I know.

The trouble with not setting clear boundaries for yourself is that you allow people to step over them and then wonder why you get upset.

Every time Tulip and I would get close, she would pull away and I would suffer an attack of rejection.

I was able to withstand these attacks whilst the honeymoon juice flowed, but after the umpteenth time, my pent-up sexual aggression burst through the seams like a volcanic eruption.

With the benefit of hindsight, I had never agreed to "wait" for Tulip.

In my own head, I had just told myself that she was now a challenge and given my perfect strike rate of seducing previous partners, this would be a walk in the park.

Now it seems like it was conscious and calculated manipulation, but in my head at that time, I was just horny, and would say anything to have this genuinely beautiful woman in my life.

The fights became more and more frequent. I started to attack her Christianity, then eventually her cultural beliefs because those were the two areas that were stopping me from getting laid.

Unfortunately, once you belittle family and faith, it's tough to come back, I assure you.

She was born and raised in Zimbabwe and the culture requirements in her village dictate that you don't get to meet the family until you're getting married.

I, on the other hand, couldn't wait to introduce her to everyone. My family immediately loved her, and she was adopted into our inner circle effortlessly.

I would have married her in a heartbeat if it wasn't for the horrendous gamophobia (fear of marriage) that I developed watching every single person in my family get divorced at least twice (and sometimes more). My Mum has had five surnames for God's sake!

We lasted thirteen months before the wheels finally came off and the relationship collapsed into a pile of dust not seen since the hydrogen bomb was dropped on Nagasaki.

At least I had proven to myself that going without sex for thirteen months wouldn't actually kill me. But talk about a dry spell.

Just call me Laban *Sahara* Ditchburn; I couldn't have been far from sprouting my own palm trees, camels, and silk traders.

The breakup destroyed me at the time. Mainly because I thought I had ruined a beautiful, smart, happy, and loving person, all because I couldn't control my evolutionary desires.

Despite the pain I was in, I never once resorted to my old vices which was a massive bonus and proved, to me at least, that I had been successful at removing the desire to escape.

Laban's random lessons:

Dr. Robert Glovers's calming and beautifully written words in *No More Mr. Nice Guy*[5] revealed to me that by not setting clear boundaries for my own needs, I created "micro-contracts"

---

[5] Robert A. Glover, *No More Mr. Nice Guy* (Philadelphia: Running Press, January 8, 2003).

with Tulip every time I did something nice for her.

The only problem with "micro-contracts" is that the person on the receiving end isn't aware of the deal. How can they ever honor the contract if they aren't in the loop?

When you do this many times over, you naturally build resentment when you get rejected, and it's only a matter of time before you burst like I did.

Making unspoken promises to people sucks—for the recipient and for you. Living and operating in integrity is better for everyone involved.

It took at least a year to heal myself from the guilt that I felt for hurting Tulip. Eventually, we were able to be civil with each other, but I'm not expecting an invite to her next birthday or the next twenty for that matter.

Learning from this experience was a major turning point for me. It made me focus on understanding myself better and being more direct and honest about what was important to me.

If you feel like asking a professional for help, a life coach is someone that I cannot recommend highly enough.

How to Meet the Person of Your Dreams

The week leading up to the 100 km run was an eventful one.

My job was going great, my training for the run had been excellent, our fundraising efforts were awesome, and I made two new connections that week that would change my life forever.

I finished work on Monday evening and was taking the lift down from the twenty-second floor when I caught the eye of a very glamorous woman. She had sparkling blue eyes and a warm, generous smile.

"Hello," I chirped. The massive grin on my face showed I was friend not foe.

"Have you been kicking ass and taking numbers today?" I boldly enquired.

She chuckled and responded as quick as a flash, "How could you tell?" Her broad Scottish accent sounded like a female version of comedic genius, Billy Connolly.

We clicked instantly and the conversation spilled into the lobby of the building.

I shared how excited I was about the upcoming run,

throwing in snippets of my recent transformation for good measure. She seemed impressed, for the most part, then shared some of her own impressive journey.

Her name was Carolyn. Originally from Scotland, she had relocated to Australia for love several years back—leaving behind family, friends, and a very successful career consulting to the UK government as a senior advisor on all matters of importance.

In her role in Australia, Carolyn was a facilitator, executive coach, and professional speaker, something I had been seriously thinking about transitioning into.

We spoke for thirty minutes before we had to part ways, but arranged a follow up meeting in a few weeks, so I could fill her in on the run and she could fill me in on what was required from a speaking point of view.

I didn't know it yet, but I had just found my first official mentor in the most unlikely of places… a lift.

The second person to change my life that week, I met on Thursday.

It was September 13, 2018.

My office was based in one of the main streets in Melbourne's bustling CBD, Queen Street.

Rather than be a lazy bum and take the public transport, I left early for an appointment 3 kms away, to enjoy the walk across town.

Dressed for success, my beautiful baby-blue sports coat

had a multi-colored pure silk pocket square that protruded from the top left-hand section of my coat.

My collared shirt was emblazoned with native Australian flowers inspired by a local indigenous artist. I had slim-fitting black tailored chinos and a brand-new pair of hazel oxfords that had the slippery leather heel replaced with a far sturdier rubber one.

The metal toe guard nailed to the front made my shoes not only fashionable, but a lethal weapon should the need arise.

In a trance of sorts, I was back into my Bradley Cooper state of *Limitless*.

I looked, felt, and acted like a million dollars—though my bank account said otherwise. Still, confidence and joy flowed through me like water.

Even the crossing signals switched from red to green whenever I neared, seemed to indicate the universe was on my side.

As I came out of the building and skipped down the steps below, I noticed a stunning silhouette of a woman walking in the distance.

Like a supermodel strutting down the runway, she placed one leg in front of the other, each step deliberately maneuvered and confidently executed.

My primal mating instincts took over and I scanned her from toe to head to ascertain a good breeding match and symmetry. She was perfect. When I got to her face, I saw she was looking straight at me, with a beautiful smile.

What happened next, I can't really explain; all I can say is I felt a supernatural force lift me a foot in the air, levitate me directly toward this glorious creature, and plonk me down in front of her, the metal in my shoes clinking as it made contact with the ground.

She looked at me as though she'd just witnessed the second coming of Christ. Before she could say anything, however, I spoke.

"Excuse me… but you are stunning."

This was delivered with the coolness of Frank Sinatra and the confidence of a thousand Spartan warriors.

"I wondered if you would go and have a drink with me some time?"

Pow! There it was—probably the greatest pick-up line ever delivered from one human being to another and it was I who got to say it.

Eat your heart out, *Elite Singles*.

"You look good, too," she said in a beautiful foreign accent.

Anna, as I found out, was three quarters Russian and one quarter Japanese.

She was born on the Island of Sakhalin, a separate island off the Russian mainland and only a few hundred kilometers from the coast of Japan.

This woman was the most naturally beautiful human being I had ever laid eyes upon, and she thought I was good looking, too?

Hang on, this is too good to be true.

Scanning the perimeter, I half expected Ashton Kutcher to burst out from behind the tree and yell, "Punk'd!"

But Ashton never came. It was real life, and I was living it, and it was really cool.

I had gone from an overweight, subservient pushover of a man to a strong, confident, cocky, and ballsy masculine man in the space of a few short years.

I had invested hundreds, if not thousands of hours learning and mastering the art of meeting the person of my dreams, and this time around, I fucking nailed it.

There was powerful chemistry crackling between the two of us and the conversation flowed effortlessly.

I held out my mobile phone and prompted her to add her number. She politely declined, citing common sense in giving her personal details to a complete stranger (charming and handsome though he may be).

I agreed and gave her mine. I repeated my ten-digit number at least half a dozen times to ensure a flawless entry, but I knew that if I didn't hear from her, I would scour the streets every day until I did.

Rather than shake hands awkwardly, we shared a warm embrace and I kissed her on the cheek, taking in her scent in the process.

She smelled just like the woman of my dreams.

Laban's random lessons:

- Get your shit together and you can win the girl.
- Good relationships take time to build.

How to Severely Injure Your Body

The lead up to the 100 km run was a disaster.

I had the responsibility of booking the accommodations for us all and due to my own error, I had booked a place nearly three hours' drive from the start line.

The extra distance meant we needed to wake up at 3 AM in order to get out the door in time. So, with all the adrenaline, excitement, and nervous energy flowing through me, I didn't sleep a wink.

The run would start with a twenty-four-hour sleep deficit.

Sam and I agreed to repeat our stick-together-to-the-end mantra, which worked well during our marathon run, but given this was 57 km further than our best effort, it would take some serious effort and teamwork.

My baby brother, Josh, and his Scottish pal, John, generously flew in from interstate the day before and decided to pull their own "all-nighter."

Enjoying time away from their families was a rare event for them and they made hay whilst the sun shone. Something they'd live to regret.

Sam's wife, Jo, arrived on Saturday.

Together, they formed the JJJ gang: Jo, Josh, and John; they were our crew. Their role was to meet Sam and I at every scheduled stop point along the trail, providing fresh clothes, food, first-aid, and false hope when required.

We posed for pre-race photos. I showed off by doing a fly kick, hoping to capture my awesomeness for posterity. As I kicked into the air, I felt something click in my right buttock, but thought nothing of it.

We joined 450 other runners at the start line, the foghorn sounded, and we set off.

The first section of the course was fairly brutal, but we made it to the first 25 km marker in three hours. Not bad considering the first quarter is almost all sand and water.

We swapped out our soaking wet shoes, socks, and shorts with fresh new kit, and headed off toward the next major stop point at 50 km.

At the halfway mark, just on seven hours, we were still in good spirits, although my right knee was starting to ache.

Enjoying a decent stop at the main rest point, we refueled on rarely cooked scotch fillet steak, soft boiled eggs, dates, potato chips, and salted water. Not necessarily in that order.

The decent weather we had enjoyed for the first half of the day disappeared behind dark black rain clouds, and the barometer dropped like the NASDAQ in 2008.

As I lifted my body off the fold out camping chair, I felt

my right leg give out.

I caught myself and managed to rebalance with the help of my brother's steady shoulder.

"You alright, bro?" he asked.

What I said and what I thought were two very different things.

"Yes, mate," I lied. "Just a knock on the knee."

The truth was I had picked up a small glute issue trying to be clever with my fly kick photo op. The additional hours spent aggravating that small injury manifested it into a large one.

Specifically, I was suffering from iliotibial band syndrome (ITB).

It's a very painful condition in which connective tissue rubs against the thigh bone.

The main symptom is acute pain between the hip and knees that worsens with activity.

That last line couldn't be more accurate if it tried.

As the heavens opened and the temperature plummeted, the pain in my knee worsened with every step.

To add insult to injury, the newly arrived rain quickly soaked the clay mud pathways and my ill-equipped footwear morphed into a fresh pair of "mud skates" to thrill the likes of Torvill and Dean.

I was sliding left and right, backward and forward. Every time I moved at an angle, the pain tunneled its way through my knee, hip and back. Every movement felt like someone had plunged a rusty prison shank into me.

Since we had raised a small fortune for a mental health charity, One in Five, completing the race was rather important. I couldn't take people's hard-earned money and then drop out mere miles from the finish line.

Ultramarathons are supposed to hurt. You're supposed to be sore at the end of the run. But at what point do you draw the line on safety?

Carrying your own hydration, food, first aid kit, and warm clothing is mandatory in runs of this length, but you can't pack for experience in unbelievably challenging conditions.

As the temperature continued to drop, so did my body temperature, electrolytes, and will to go on.

I drank water like a fish to avoid dehydration, but in doing so, I depleted myself of key salts and vital minerals.

One of the main side effects when depleting the body… you decrease your body's ability to generate heat.

Sam was starting to experience similar effects, but at least he could run ahead for a kilometer or two and then wait for me, producing his own body warmth to keep him going.

At its slowest, our pace went from seven minutes per kilometer to fifty-two minutes per kilometer.

You could probably crawl faster than that, even on the slippery mud.

That pace meant an estimated finish time of eighty-five

hours, more than sixty hours past the cut-off!

Sam stayed patient with me, but I could see the colder and wetter he got, the less benevolent about the situation he was getting.

We arrived together at the 86 km checkpoint, and I broke down again. The brutality of what I was experiencing was taking a huge emotional toll on me and I just wanted the pain to stop.

I had been moving non-stop for fourteen hours at that point, seven hours of which I was dealing with pain so severe I was on the brink of flaking out more than once.

No amount of practiced gratitude, positivity, or encouragement from the sideline could motivate me to keep going at that point.

I was done.

Our crew was experiencing their own challenges.

Josh and John's decision to not sleep the previous night was starting to cause rifts in their previously sound relationship and their ability to function as a support crew diminished dramatically.

Jo stood back and watched in horror as they fought over which socks to bring out—a sleep-deprived, full-blown argument over nothing.

The last thing you need, want, or hope when you're in that much pain is for the people entrusted to look after you to fight. I snapped in anger, "Can you two please SHUT THE

FUCK UP?"

They immediately stopped their quibbling and refocused their attention to the walking dead (that was me).

Josh pushed a small packet of triangle-shaped, industrial-strength pain pills into my hand as Sam finally coaxed me into getting up and persisting onwards.

The sooner we finished, the sooner the pain would end—at least that was his sales line.

I swallowed three of the pills with a mouthful of home-made bone broth and chased it down with some frog-shaped milk-chocolate. The frog had been broken into quarters, to be rationed for the last crucial kilometers.

Rationing was for cowards I told myself, and in a few short seconds, the frogs went the way of the dodo: #Extinct.

It may sound gross, but the combination of sweet, salty, creamy, and savory tasted like paradise and gave me a much-needed burst of morale, albeit temporarily.

I gave Sam permission to run ahead; I even told him half a dozen times to go on without me. He refused to ditch me but continued to run ahead for a little bit, to get warm. He'd wait for me to hobble along like the hunchback of Notre Dame, the only thing differentiating me from Quasimodo was a race bib and head torch.

In one period of solitude, the painkillers kicked in.

Rather than doing their job as pain relief, they just exacerbated my already heavy fatigue and triggered a series of hallucinations that included unicorns, My Little Ponies, and a few other characters that wouldn't be out of place in a *Lord of the Rings* movie.

You might think it enjoyable to relive an acid trip, but I was in more pain than I thought humanly possible, so the fun side was lost on me.

Just when I thought I couldn't be any more miserable, the hail started.

The southerly wind whipped ice and sleet into my face and cut into my flushed cheeks like a blunt cut throat razor blade. My teeth started chattering like a Bren gun at Normandy on D-Day and I was genuinely thinking death could be an option.

We were positioned between the last checkpoint and the finish line. The thought of backpedalling was too much to contemplate; I only had the one option and that was to finish this motherfucker.

With less than 3 km to go, you would think that your spirits would be high, and the thought of completion would outweigh any negative thoughts, but I couldn't have been more despondent if I tried.

My body, layered with as many clothes as I could find, was still frozen deep to its core, and being that cold caused its own pain response.

I had been awake for forty hours eight straight and easily in the most pain I have ever experienced. I'm sure I'll ruffle a few feathers here, but I reckon the pain must've been close to what women must experience during childbirth.

Sam's amazingly calm and measured temperament had long since disappeared and he was well within his rights to be upset.

If you have bone protruding through your flesh, it's easy to empathize with someone, but when the injury is hidden, it's only a matter of time before people get ticked off.

I liken it to what someone might experience when dealing with chronic fatigue or a family member with depression.

But rather than lambaste me, Sam dug deep one more time and shouted words of encouragement.

"C'mon, Labes, you and I have got this!" It was more pleading than confirming. "Think about how good this will be!"

I went deep within my soul and begged whoever was listening to give me the strength to finish.

I channeled my own fifty shades of grey and slapped my face with enough force that I snapped into action. I bit down on my lip and swung my injured leg out and around.

With the light starting to dim on my battery-powered head torch and my body's own fuel cells finally depleting themselves, Sam and I crossed that damned finish line hand-in-hand, just like we'd promised each other.

An emotional release burst from us all as I collapsed into my brother's arms. Josh's chest, swollen with pride, created a warm embrace that freed us to weep with relief and joy.

John entered a triangular embrace with Sam and Jo. Perfect

strangers only hours before, now lifelong companions.

Eighteen hours, fifty-five minutes, and forty-seven seconds of the most grueling, painful, and exhilarating experience you could imagine.

Still to this day, the hardest and best thing I've ever done for myself—not for any other reason than it unlocked something deep within my core about what was actually possible, physically. It also accessed a part of my brain that no longer had a ceiling on what I believe is now achievable in my life.

Arriving back at our accommodations three arduous hours later, I sat under a hot shower for forty minutes, slowly bringing a semblance of warmth back into my body. I was utterly depleted in every sense but had enough left to crack a huge toothy smile, because I still had something even more exciting to look forward to.

By now you've likely noticed the recurring theme of going on dates soon after each run. Well, this time was no different, as I had made arrangements to meet the Russian stunner, Anna, on Monday evening.

After spending the majority of the morning learning how to walk again, I prettied myself up and headed into the city to go on my date.

Usually broken amateur ultramarathoners spend a week on a couch recovering, but Monday evening was the only time slot that we could meet and there was no way on God's green earth I was going to delay it any further.

We met at a beautiful rooftop bar called QT, which is one way to describe Anna as she walked in.

Actually, drop dead gorgeous wouldn't do her justice. She was even more beautiful than I remembered and the warmth that she exuded as we embraced would melt even the coldest of broken hearts.

What started that evening was a romance that still burns white-hot to this day. To steal from Mark Victor Hansen, Anna is my Twin Flame. We burn brighter together.

Anna is the woman I knew I wanted to meet my whole life but was beginning to think it would never happen. Thank God for staying patient and trusting this process.

The universe made me wait until I had done the work, looked hard enough at myself and truly began to love who I was. Then, and only then, was I able to be loved.

Our time together has been the most enjoyable, loving, fun, uplifting, positive, and educational of any of my previous years on earth.

We've had our moments for sure and there's still much work to be done, but we're on that path together. And, hot dang… it's so much better with a partner that you get on well with.

Laban's random lessons:

- I can't believe how much crying I have done in this book!
- Do the work and you'll get the rewards.
- The average caloric load on a 100 km race is around 10,000 calories. That's thirty-eight Big Macs, in case you're wondering. It's also one of the few times in your life that you will be able to outrun a diet. So go nuts, you have my blessing.

BET ON YOU—THE FINAL CHAPTER

So, Laban, thanks for sharing your awesome, outrageous and sometimes highly unbelievable stories, but what's the magic bullet takeaway for all of this? How do you sum up all your random lessons?

Well, I'm so very glad you asked.

i. During my own lowest point, I sought help from the gambler's helpline.

For you, it might be the suicide helpline, Alcoholics Anonymous, Narcotics Anonymous, Overeaters Anonymous, Lifeline, child protection helpline, spousal abuse helpline, a trusted neighbour, or even the national emergency phone number.

Whatever it is, make that call.

Whatever your situation right now, no matter how desperate or helpless it might seem, ask for help.

And ask for help so that you may remain strong, not so that you appear weak, and keep asking for help until you get it.

Trying to make rational decisions during times of heightened stress is almost impossible.

Even the stoics agree that it's almost always worse in our heads.

> *"We suffer more often in imagination than in reality."*
> —Seneca

We need that space to get sane thoughts back into our head and reaching out for help will allow you that precious time.

Plus we always feel better after we've gotten it off our chest.

ii. Making a decision to improve yourself is the best decision you'll ever make.

Sitting on that decision and waiting for someone to rescue you is the worst decision you can make.

No one is coming to save you.

My decision was motivated purely by the fact that my life wasn't fun anymore. So, I took massive action to bring some of that joy back into my life.

Work out your main motivation. Why do you want to improve?

It may be health (mental, physical, or emotional), well-being, meeting the person of your dreams, starting your own business, or any number of other things. Once you know it, act.

iii. Own your flaws.

First things first, a flaw isn't even a flaw. It's part of your character and it helps define your uniqueness.

However, when you burden others with your misery, 90% of people don't care, and the rest are GLAD it's happening to you!

So, stop whining about it and start taking ownership of your fuck ups, mistakes, broken promises, bad ideas, terrible relationships, and whatever else belongs on this list.

I'll go first.

I was a fat, lazy, drunken gambler-a-holic who used drugs, sex, and pornography to get through my days.

See, it's not that hard.

I speak so candidly about it now because it holds no power over me. I've taken back any fear of being outed for my past behaviors. The sooner you acknowledge that you're not perfect, you'll allow other people to open up and share their stories with you, thus normalizing this shit.

Bill Cosby, one of the world's most successful comedians and television stars, was, on paper, the perfect person.

He pooh-poohed other comedians use of profanity and all the while, (allegedly) committed some of the worst sex crimes most of us have ever heard of!

So, unless you're Dr. Huxtable, maybe go easy on your past wrongdoings. We all fuck up from time to time. It's what we learn from those experiences that really matters.

And honestly, it's almost always fun talking about the crazy shit in my life that nearly killed me.

It gives me the drive to do better, be better, and inspire others to be brave.

iv. One thing I've figured out about real life is that most people, in general, have little real clue what they are talking about.

Stop accepting everything at face value and dig a little deeper.

I'm including professors, doctors, scientists, politicians, Bill Gates and anyone else who has a platform from which to spout.

How do I know this?

Because I have little real clue about what I'm talking about.

In fact, the more I learn about the world, the more I realize I know fuck all about it, but I do know when I'm being lied to.

The sheer amount of bullshit that flows forth from the mouths of people is astounding. It's up to us to figure out exactly what is the truth and what isn't.

Remember, earlier in the book I talked about the twenty medical professionals that all separately said, "There's nothing you can do about your health issue, it's a genetic disorder."

You remember this?

Well here's what I would say if I was in their position.

"Honestly, Mr. Ditchburn, the real answer is that we don't know what is possible and what is not these days. The medication we have been trained to prescribe will relieve your symptoms, but at what cost, we honestly have no idea. The pills you consume every day seem to be ok, but mucking with six millions years of evolution may cause long- or short-term damage."

Now that statement requires zero ego and absolute humility, and from what I can tell, it's rare to see in this day and age. It might be rare, but it's bloody necessary.

People are craving the truth in a world currently so misleading it's hard to stay on top.

But, admitting that you don't know something but are willing to try and find out, naturally endears people to you. They are way more likely to trust you now and in the future. Your impact when you DO figure something out, is magnified by a number I can't actually quantify—but it's big.

This process of approaching life has also given me perspective on other people's opinions.

I'm now way more open-minded to the fact that I might not be right.

Incidentally, it creates a drive to actually see and do things for yourself.

I recently ran a 50 km (30 miles) ultramarathon and I did 100% of the event on zero carbs or sugar.

Now that may not mean anything to those who don't follow the sport, but most people, with their knowledge of how the body works, would argue what I achieved is impossible.

Maybe you thought that, too.

Well, I just proved that it's not, so let's get on with being far more open-minded; let's challenge the status quo and actually find out for ourselves what is, in fact, possible.

Mark Twain once said, "Whenever you find yourself on the side of the majority, it is time to reform (or pause and reflect)."

v. Whilst in conversation with anyone, become an active listener. Focus on what's being said rather than trying to formulate what you want to say next.

I've conducted more than one hundred hour-long podcast interviews with some of the most interesting people on the planet. It's shown me first-hand the value of asking open questions, shutting up and listening.

Don't worry, you'll get your opportunity to contribute… and patience is a helluva drug.

vi. Enter every single interaction with a "What value can I add to this person's life?"

Seeing someone's face light up when you genuinely ask them how they are is one of the great gifts we receive in life.

Make decisions for yourself, not for someone else.

Ask yourself, "Am I making this decision for me or am I doing this for the approval or validation of someone else?"

Another great question to ask is, "How does this decision

impact other people?"

What are the intended (and unintended) outcomes of making a decision for someone else?

Am I giving up (insert behaviour that doesn't serve you) for me or am I doing this to appease my family?

Because doing it solely for someone else, always leads toward resentment, frustration, and inevitably, failure.

Once you know the answer to this, then you can decide how you would like to proceed.

vii. If you keep telling yourself that something is impossible, how the hell do you ever expect to actually do it?

Negative self-talk could be one of the worst habits we humans have.

Create a version of the "Swear Jar" in your home or place of work. Only instead of putting $1 in for profanity, put $1 for any negative self-talk.

Start catching yourself with the "I can't" or "I could never" language and swap it with "I will", "I can," or "I am."

Focus on incorporating more of the seven virtues of faith, hope, charity, justice, prudence, temperance, and fortitude by replacing (one by one) the seven deadly sins (gluttony, greed, sloth, pride, envy, lust & wrath)

***

I used to be a gambling man; in some ways, I still am—because I'm betting on me… and I'm betting on you.

I'm betting that by conquering your demons, fostering an abundance mindset, and developing your spirituality, you will win at this thing called life.

As you begin to take a closer look at yourself, I suggest you do the same: bet on yourself.

Bet. On. You.

You are an unrepeatable miracle.

Bet on you.

You are unique.

Bet on you.

Most people die at age twenty-five, but don't get buried until they're sixty-five.

Bet on you.

Because you're a winner.

You are a winner.

ABOUT THE AUTHOR

A child badly affected by divorce, Laban Ditchburn sought validation and escapism in all the wrong places.

But through self-discovery and a ton of hard work, he conquered the full gamut of addiction—alcohol, sex, gambling, drugs, and negative self-talk. He dropped sixty pounds of body fat, added thirty pounds of muscle, and put his "incurable" auto-immune disease into remission.

Today, he defines the word transformation.

He is physically, mentally, spiritually, and emotionally in charge of his own destiny and his journey continues to inspire those ready to change their lives. An exemplar and a revolutionary, he revels in unabashedly sharing what he's learned: how to conquer the demons you don't know you have, and how to be unstoppable in getting to where you want to be.

These days he gets his fix from the madness of ultramarathons, and the demolition of a hot carnivore BBQ!

Laban is living his purpose and works as a writer and inspirer, and hosts the *Become Your Own Superhero* podcast.

He lives in Australia with the woman of his dreams, Anna. ❤

Some Translations:

In the course of this book, you may have happened upon a word or two that caused you to pause and question just what in the heck I was talking about. Chances are good that word was Australian (or British) slang. Here are a few definitions, to help you out.

Bloody – an expression of emphasis.

Bugger all – slang for "very little" or "nothing at all."

Buggered – slang for "not quite sure."

Cops an absolute hiding – slang for "got beaten up extensively"

Codswallop –slang for "nonsense."

Flog – slang for "to sell," with the implication that it's being sold quickly or cheaply.

Fossicking – "to search about, rummage."

Frothies – slang for "beer."

Firkle – slang for "tinkering in a workshop."

Lollipop sign – a circular sign on a pole.

Mahjongers – a made-up word for people who play Mahjong.

Ridgy-didge – slang for "genuine, authentic, legitimate, etc."

Shonky – something of dubious integrity or legality; "unreliable or unsound."

Wow, what a ride, huh?

I hope you loved *Bet on You* as much as I loved writing it.

For those who want just a little more, I'd like you to have something extra as a token of my appreciation (and something I wish someone had shown me years ago)!

Head on over to **www.labanditchburn.com/publications/bet-on-you/my-gift-to-you** where you can gain access to the following:

1. Exclusive video content explaining how I used the carnivore lifestyle to supercharge my mental health, creativity, athleticism, libido, and all the other wonderful benefits of being healthy.
2. Real-life examples of how I overcame the fear of rejection and used this new skill set to meet, interview, and become friends with some of the most inspiring people on the planet (and how you can too).
3. How to best manage friends and family when you decide to improve your life (and upset all their plans for you).
4. And finally, three questions that you must know the answer to, if you are to understand your reason for being on this planet.

Here's to a heathier, happier you!

Twig – informal for "understand" or to realize something.

Pash – slang for "kissing passionately."

Wanker – vulgar slang for "a contemptible person."

Very Helpful Reading:

Since 2017, I've consumed nearly 500 book titles and all of them have impacted me in some, way shape or form, however here are a few highlights

A Fat Lot of Good by Dr. Peter Brukner

Lies My Doctor Told Me by Dr. Ken Berry

Carnivore Cure by Judy Cho

Toxic Legacy How the Weedkiller Glyphosate Is Destroying Our Health and the Environment by Dr. Stephanie Seneff

No More Mr. Nice Guy: A Proven Plan for Getting What You Want in Love, Sex and Life by Dr. Robert Glover

The Ultimate Zig Ziglar Library by Zig Ziglar

12 Rules for Life: An Antidote to Chaos by Dr. Jordan Peterson

Set Your Voice Free: How to Get the Singing or Speaking Voice You Want by Roger Love

We Are One by Vanessa Broers

Facing Codependence: What It Is, Where It Comes from, How It Sabotages Our Lives by Pia Mellody

You've Got To Be Hungry by Les Brown

Can't Hurt Me by David Goggins (Audible version best!)

Why We Get Sick: The Hidden Epidemic at the Root of Most Chronic Disease - and How to Fight It by Benjamin Bikman, Ph.D.

The Fat of the Land by Vilhjalmur Stefansson

How to Eat the Elephant by Ann Sheybani

Legacy by James Kerr

Think and Grow Rich by Napoleon Hill

Models by Mark Manson

No More Mr. Nice Guy by Dr. Robert Glover

Forgive for Good by Dr. Fred Luskin

The Go-Giver by Bob Burg and John David Mann

Chicken Soup for the Soul by Jack Canfield and Mark Victor Hansen

Men Are from Mars, Women Are from Venus by Dr. John Gray

Cry Like a Man by Jason Wilson

The Resilience Project by Hugh van Cuylenburg

Messages from the Masters by Dr. Brian Weiss

Optimal Outcomes by Jennifer Goldman-Wetzler, Ph.D.

Bluefishing by Steve Sims

The Rational Male by Rollo Tomassi

The Art of Influence by Chris Widener

Twelve Pillars by Jim Rohn and Chris Widener*Never Fly Solo* by Lt. Col. Robert "Waldo" Waldman

Legendary by Tommy Breedlove

Iconic by Scott McKain

It Starts with Passion by Keith Abraham

Click! The Competitive Edge by Dan Schaefer, Ph.D.

Journeys On The Edge by Walt Hampton

What to Say When You Talk to Yourself by Shad Helmstetter

177 Mental Toughness Secrets of the World Class by Steve Siebold

I'm No Hero by Capt. Charlie Plumb

The Strangest Secret by Earl Nightingale

Three Feet from Gold by Greg Reid and Sharon Lechter, CPA

Molly Parkin News Articles:

www.express.co.uk/dayandnight/11202/Naughty-Molly-on-crest-of-a-wave

www.walesonline.co.uk/news/wales-news/molly-reveals-hot-affair-las-2237016

www.dailymail.co.uk/home/you/article-468229/Good-golly-Ms-Molly.html

Step-Back-Think anti-violence campaign:

www.labanditchburn.com/media/step-back-think

Laban's Highly Recommended Additional Resources

www.labanditchburn.com/additional-resources-for-bet-on-you/